Enlightened

by the Lord

Abby,

May your heart be

Enlightened by the Lord's

Love, Stacie Neabell

1

Ephesians 1:18

Enlightened

by the Lord

A Journal for when He speaks

Written by: Staci Holland Pealock
Illustrated by: Mikaela Peachey Pealock

ISBN-13: 978-0692803714 (Staci Holland Pealock)
ISBN-10:0692803718

Printed in the United States of America

All scriptures obtained through Biblegateway.com

© AMP - Amplified
© ERV - Easy-to-Read Version
© ESV - English Standard Version
© HCSB - Holman Christian Standard Bible
© NASB - New American Standard Bible
© NIV - New International Versions
© NLT - New Living Translation
© KJV - King James Versions
© MSG - The Message
© NKJV - New King James Version
© ISV - International Standard Version
© CEV - Contemporary English Version

Dedication

This book is dedicated to my parents *Jimmie Marie Taylor* and *Robert Gerald Holland*. Both my parents are precious to me. They gave me life and both have loved me deeply from their hearts. The woman I am today is because of who they are. May God be the blessing to them as they have been to me. Thank you Mama and Daddy!

Acknowledgements:

To my sweet Lord for meeting with me each morning and speaking to my heart. Often times I was fretful and unsure that I would even have something to write. During those times you gently reminded me the words come from thee, not me! I Love You ~♥~

To my precious husband Todd. Your unwavering support and encouragement blesses my heart every day. I love the way you love me. Thank you from the bottom of my heart.

To my precious Friends that helped me edit, format and fine tune this book. Deborah Holley, Betty Perry, Kathy Swick and Wanda Tate - you are AWESOME! Thank you!

Front Cover designed by my son, Andrew Pealock. You may contact him at ampmediastudios@gmail.com.

Introduction

This book was birthed from a secret place that I enjoyed with the Lord for many years. When He would speak to my heart, I would write down His precious words. In 2015 the Lord directed me to share publicly what He had always shared with me privately. This was a huge step for me, but one I took in obedience to the Lord. I would post His precious word on facebook and share with my friends. Then as the year went on, it became apparent to me that a book was forming from the pages. It was a joint effort with my creative and artsy Daughter-in-Love Mikaela, as we added the graphics for the "Staci-isms" which you may choose to color. Here's what is in store for your journey. The week begins on Sunday with a "Staci-ism". Monday through Friday you're reading words spoken to me from the heart of our Father, with scripture included. On Saturday you have time to reflect and write what the Lord is speaking to your heart. It is my desire that over the next 365 days, you will enjoy a deeper more meaningful relationship with the Lord. May you be enlightened by His love, through His grace and with His presence each and every day.

For His Glory,

Sista Staci Pealock

you can't GO wrong doing Right

My child,

I am your fresh start. I have the power to make all things new. You only have to believe in me and you will experience my power working through you to accomplish my will in your life. Seek me, Know me, and you will find me! My will can show you The Way, The Truth and The Life I desire for you.

I Love You ~♥~

Romans 8:11 (ESV)
If the Spirit of him who raised Jesus from the dead dwells in you, he who raised Christ Jesus from the dead will also give life to your mortal bodies through his Spirit who dwells in you.

Matthew 7:7-12 (NKJV)
"Ask, and it will be given to you; seek, and you will find; knock, and it will be opened to you. 8 For everyone who asks receives, and he who seeks finds, and to him who knocks it will be opened. 9 Or what man is there among you who, if his son asks for bread, will give him a stone? 10 Or if he asks for a fish, will he give him a serpent? 11 If you then, being evil, know how to give good gifts to your children, how much more will your Father who is in heaven give good things to those who ask Him! 12 Therefore, whatever you want men to do to you, do also to them, for this is the Law and the Prophets."

John 14:6 (NIV)
Jesus answered, "I am the way and the truth and the life. No one comes to the Father except through me."

My child,

As you walk with me, I will give you step-by-step instructions. I call you to my divine order. You will not find peace trying to put your life together by your plans. Don't get in a hurry trying to know every step to take before it's time. When you walk with me, your steps will be made by faith and I will not let you stumble. Trust me, walk it out one step at a time!

I Love You ~♥~

Psalm 119:133 (NLT)
Guide my steps by your word, so I will not be overcome by evil.

Proverbs 16:9 (NLT)
We can make our plans, but the Lord determines our steps.

Psalm 37:23 (NLT)
The Lord directs the steps of the godly. He delights in every detail of their lives.

My child,

It's time to move. You've been on-the-mark, getting-set, and now it's time to go. I see you're in a comfort zone and fear of failure is holding you there. It's time to move away from that place of defeat. I have freedom to offer you, and if you allow me to work through you, then VICTORY is guaranteed!

I Love You ~♥~

Philippians 3:14 (KJV)
I press toward the mark for the prize of the high calling of God in Christ Jesus.

John 15:16 (NLT)
You didn't choose me. I chose you. I appointed you to go and produce lasting fruit, so that the Father will give you whatever you ask for, using my name.

Galatians 5:1 (ESV)
For freedom Christ has set us free; stand firm therefore, and do not submit again to a yoke of slavery.

My child,

You are beautiful! I created you with all your special qualities. I want you to view yourself through my eyes. Eyes that are full of love and compassion for you. I am on your side - you are not alone! Please allow others to see the beauty I've created in you. Arise and shine for you are mine!

I Love You ~♥~

Psalm 139:13-14 (ESV)
For you formed my inward parts; you knitted me together in my mother's womb. I praise you, for I am fearfully and wonderfully made. Wonderful are your works; my soul knows it very well.

Psalm 119:18 (NLT)
Open my eyes to see the wonderful truths in your instructions.

Psalm 118:6 (ESV)
The LORD is on my side; I will not fear. What can man do to me?

Isaiah 60:1 (ESV)
Arise, shine, for your light has come, and the glory of the LORD has risen upon you.

My child,

Why do you worry about what people think of you? It's not what they think that matters, it's what I know to be true about you. I know you from the inside out. When people treat or speak negatively of you, do not defend yourself. I am the Lord, your God, your defender. I will fight for you! My words defeat the accuser of my children! You will always be victorious if you remain quiet when under attack, in your silence the enemy cannot locate you! I will defend you and defeat the enemy.

I Love you ~♥~

2 Corinthians 1:20-22 (NLT)
For all of God's promises have been fulfilled in Christ with a resounding "Yes!" And through Christ, our "Amen" (which means "Yes") ascends to God for his glory. 21 It is God who enables us, along with you, to stand firm for Christ. He has commissioned us, 22 and he has identified us as his own by placing the Holy Spirit in our hearts as the first installment that guarantees everything he has promised us.

Exodus 14:13-14 (ESV)
And Moses said to the people, "Fear not, stand firm, and see the salvation of the Lord, which he will work for you today. For the Egyptians whom you see today, you shall never see again. 14 The Lord will fight for you, and you have only to be silent."

My Child,

_____
_____
_____
_____
_____
_____
_____
_____
_____
_____
_____
_____
_____
_____
_____
_____
_____
_____
_____
_____
_____
_____
_____
_____
_____
_____
_____
_____
_____

I Love You

~~

My child,

Today I am asking you to watch for my favor. You are my child and I love you! I want to bless your life abundantly. Many times you miss my blessings because you're too busy to notice how I'm moving in your midst. Today, I am asking you to slow down so you will notice my special presence and favor all around you. I am here with you!

I Love you ~♥~

Proverbs 3:3-4 (NLT)
Never let loyalty and kindness leave you! Tie them around your neck as a reminder. Write them deep within your heart. 4 Then you will find favor with both God and people, and you will earn a good reputation.

Zephaniah 3:17 (ESV)
The LORD your God is in your midst, a mighty one who will save; he will rejoice over you with gladness; he will quiet you by his love; he will exult over you with loud singing.

My child,

This world is not your home. Watch out, be alert and don't become too comfortable. I am calling you to a higher standard of living in my Spirit. When you choose to separate from worldliness, you increase your effectiveness for my Kingdom. The people that I place in your path need you to be strong and filled with my power! This will lead them in the right direction, helping them to find their final destination: A Heavenly Home!

I Love You ~♥~

1 Peter 2:11 (MSG)
Friends, this world is not your home, so don't make yourselves cozy in it. Don't indulge your ego at the expense of your soul.

Romans 12:2 (KJV)
And be not conformed to this world: but be ye transformed by the renewing of your mind, that ye may prove what is that good, and acceptable, and perfect, will of God.

Hebrews 13:14 (NLT)
For this world is not our permanent home; we are looking forward to a home yet to come.

My child,

I hear you say, "All I want to be is happy." You say, "If I only had a different job, I'd be happy or if I had a new car, home, or if I looked different, I'd be happy." This is just not true because you cannot find happiness there. When you seek Joy in me, then you will truly be happy! I AM Enough!

I Love You ~♥~

Matthew 6:33 (NLT)
Seek the Kingdom of God above all else, and live righteously, and he will give you everything you need.

Nehemiah 8:10 (NLT)
...The Joy of the Lord is your strength.

My child,

Whatever you're seeking you will find; Please seek me! If you could conceive and believe how much I love you, then you would receive from me. Your striving in the world would turn into abiding in me. Trust me all the way.

I Love You ~♥~

Mark 11:24 (NLT)
I tell you, you can pray for anything, and if you believe that you've received it, it will be yours.

John 15:4 (NASB)
Abide in Me, and I in you. As the branch cannot bear fruit of itself unless it abides in the vine, so neither can you unless you abide in me.

Proverbs 3:5-6 (KJV)
Trust in the Lord with all thine heart; and lean not unto thine own understanding. 6 In all thy ways acknowledge him, and he shall direct thy paths.

My child,

I go before you clearing the way. My path is perfect for you. When you encounter obstacles, stop and seek my face for direction. There is no need to look to the right or the left trying to navigate through without me. Life can be like a traffic jam; you have to sit, be patient and let it clear. When you try and MANeuver around, that is when you become anxious and aggravated; just stay still. All will clear out and you will be able to move forward again.

 I Love You ~♥~

Luke 3:5 (NIV)
Every valley shall be filled in, every mountain and hill made low. The crooked roads shall become straight, the rough ways smooth.

Psalm 16:8 (NIV)
I keep my eyes always on the LORD. With him at my right hand, I will not be shaken.

Philippians 4:6-7 (NKJV)
Be anxious for nothing, but in everything by prayer and supplication, with thanksgiving, let your requests be made known to God; 7 and the peace of God, which surpasses all understanding, will guard your hearts and minds through Christ Jesus.

Psalm 46:10 (NLT)
"Be still, and know that I am God! I will be honored by every nation. I will be honored throughout the world."

My Child,

_____

_____

_____

_____

_____

_____

_____

_____

_____

_____

_____

_____

_____

_____

_____

_____

_____

_____

_____

_____

_____

_____

_____

_____

_____

_____

_____

I Love You

~♥~

god
is
large
and in
charge

My child,

I know you. I have called you by name. In your time of trouble and distress, look to me. I am waiting with arms open wide and my heart full of compassion and love for you. You can never disappoint me. Don't allow your disappointment in yourself to separate from me. When these troubling times arise, run to me not from me. I will steady your feet and set you on the right path.

I Love you ~♥~

Psalm 107:19-21 (ESV)
Then they cried to the Lord in their trouble, and he delivered them from their distress. 20 He sent out his word and healed them, and delivered them from their destruction. 21 Let them thank the Lord for his steadfast love, for his wondrous works to the children of man!
Psalm 145:18-19 (AMP)
The Lord is near to all who call on Him, To all who call on Him in truth (without guile). 19 He will fulfill the desire of those who fear and worship Him [with awe-inspired reverence and obedience]; He also will hear their cry and will save them.

James 4:1-3 (MSG)
Where do you think all these appalling wars and quarrels come from? Do you think they just happen? Think again. They come about because you want your own way, and fight for it deep inside yourselves. You lust for what you don't have and are willing to kill to get it. You want what isn't yours and will risk violence to get your hands on it. 2-3You wouldn't think of just asking God for it, would you? And why not? Because you know you'd be asking for what you have no right to. You're spoiled children, each wanting your own way.

My child,

If only you could see yourself as I see you. Then your heart would be filled with Peace, Joy and Contentment. It's time to stop being critical of yourself and embrace how I made you. You are my MASTERPIECE! No longer will you look through eyes of defeat and despair. Lift up your head and be the Overcomer I call you to be.

I Love You ~♥~

John 16:33 (NLT)
I have told you all this so that you may have peace in me. Here on earth you will have many trials and sorrows. But take heart, because I have overcome the world.

Revelation 12:11 (NLT)
And they have defeated him by the blood of the Lamb and by their testimony. And they did not love their lives so much that they were afraid to die.

Ephesians 2:10 (NLT)
For we are God's masterpiece. He has created us anew in Christ Jesus, so we can do the good things he planned for us long ago.

My child,

I will never ask you to carry your burdens. Give them to me and I will carry them for you. Your worries only weigh you down and keep you from living on the lighter side of life. I came to give you the blessed life. Removing your burdens makes room for my blessings!

I Love You ~♥~

Ephesians 1:3 (NLT)
All praise to God, the Father of our Lord Jesus Christ, who has blessed us with every spiritual blessing in the heavenly realms because we are united with Christ.

Deuteronomy 2:7 (NLT)
For the Lord your God has blessed you in everything you have done. He has watched your every step through this great wilderness. During these forty years, the Lord your God has been with you, and you have lacked nothing.'"

My child,

When you were younger you played a game called "Follow the Leader." This game involved watching the one in front of you and doing just as the leader did. It's time for you to once again "Follow the Leader." Let me lead you, and you do as I do. It may not always be easy to walk in my ways, but I assure you, great is your reward when you follow my steps. Stop following the fallen faulty flesh, it's time to model your Master!

 I Love you ~♥~

Romans 12:2 (KJV)
And be not conformed to this world: but be ye transformed by the renewing of your mind, that ye may prove what is good, and acceptable, and the perfect, will of God.

2 Corinthians 3:18 (HSCB)
We all, with unveiled faces, are looking as in a mirror at the glory of the Lord and are being transformed into the same image from glory to glory; this is from the Lord who is the Spirit

My child,

Today I am speaking directly to the heart of my daughters. I want you to embrace the pattern that I made for you. You are fashioned by my hands, and that never goes out of style. If you will allow me full access to your heart, I will heal your brokenness, and restore the joy of your salvation. I've called and chosen YOU, how will you answer me? Believe me, YOU are beautiful!

I Love You ~♥~

Psalm 119:73 (NASB)
Your hands made me and fashioned me; Give me understanding, that I may learn Your commandments.

Proverbs 23:26 (NASB)
Give me your heart, my (daughter), And let your eyes delight in my ways.

Psalm 51:12 (ESV)
Restore to me the joy of your salvation, and uphold me with a willing spirit.

My Child,

I Love You

Dont fall to PIECES, listen to what PEACE says

My child,

Time is in my hands. I see you running around, always feeling like you're never going to catch up. During these moments, slow down and call upon my name, and I will answer you. Learn to enjoy the journey that I place you on, and without hesitation you'll reach your destination!

I Love You ~♥~

Psalm 31:15 (NIV)
My times are in your hands; deliver me from the hands of my enemies, from those who pursue me.

Psalm 145: 17-19 (NLT)
The LORD is righteous in everything he does; he is filled with kindness. 18 The LORD is close to all who call on him, yes, to all who call on him in truth. 19 He grants the desires of those who fear him; he hears their cries for help and rescues them.

Deuteronomy 2:7 (NASB)
"For the LORD your God has blessed you in all that you have done; He has known your wanderings through this great wilderness These forty years the LORD your God has been with you; you have not lacked a thing.'"

My child,

I've called you out of the darkness into my marvelous light. The loneliness you feel is because the darkness separates you from me. I expose the darkness to expel it from your life. I do this not to hurt you, but to heal you! I love you too much to leave you in that place of despair. Trust me, you deserve to live in the light with me.

I Love You ~♥~

1 Peter 2:9 (NLT)
But you are not like that, for you are a chosen people. You are royal priests, a holy nation, God's very own possession. As a result, you can show others the goodness of God, for he called you out of the darkness into his wonderful light.

1 Corinthians 4:5 (NIV)
Therefore judge nothing before the appointed time; wait until the Lord comes. He will bring to light what is hidden in darkness and will expose the motives of the heart. At that time each will receive their praise from God.

1 John 6-7 (NIV)
If we say that we have fellowship with Him and yet walk in the darkness, we lie and do not practice the truth; 7 but if we walk in the Light as He Himself is in the Light, we have fellowship with one another, and the blood of Jesus His Son cleanses us from all sin.

Isaiah 43:1 (NIV)
But now, this is what the LORD says-- he who created you, Jacob, he who formed you, Israel: "Do not fear, for I have redeemed you; I have summoned you by name; you are mine."

My child,

My love for you is immeasurable and is freely given to you. I love you unconditionally, regardless of what you do right or wrong. My love never changes. In a world where you can at times experience changes moment by moment, rest assured my love is constant and never changes. My love will never fail you, trust me! Seek my love to fill your heart, and you will never endure emptiness again.

I Love You ~♥~

Romans 5:5 (NLT)
5 And this hope will not lead to disappointment. For we know how dearly God loves us, because he has given us the Holy Spirit to fill our hearts with his love.

Ephesians 3:14-21 (NLT)
When I think of all this, I fall to my knees and pray to the Father, 15 the Creator of everything in heaven and on earth. 16 I pray that from his glorious, unlimited resources he will empower you with inner strength through his Spirit. 17 Then Christ will make his home in your hearts as you trust in him. Your roots will grow down into God's love and keep you strong. 18 And may you have the power to understand, as all God's people should, how wide, how long, how high, and how deep his love is. 19 May you experience the love of Christ, though it is too great to understand fully. Then you will be made complete with all the fullness of life and power that comes from God. 20 Now all glory to God, who is able, through his mighty power at work within us, to accomplish infinitely more than we might ask or think. 21 Glory to him in the church and in Christ Jesus through all generations forever and ever! Amen.

My child,

It is I that placed you here, it is I that brought you forth to be on earth for such a time as this. It is I that has placed divine destiny inside of you. But the choice is yours to make. Are you going to continue to believe the spoken words of man over your life? I tell you, you were not an accident, surprise or illegitimate. You must stop believing this lie of man, and choose life in me! Today, I declare that you will no longer follow the words of man, but this day you will follow my Word, and I tell you my truth will set you free!

I Love You ~♥~

Esther 4:14 (NIV)
"For if you remain silent at this time, relief and deliverance for the Jews will arise from another place, but you and your father's family will perish. And who knows but that you have come to your royal position for such a time as this?"

Joshua 24:14-16 (NASB)
"Now, therefore, fear the LORD and serve Him in sincerity and truth; and put away the gods which your fathers served beyond the River and in Egypt, and serve the LORD. 15 "If it is disagreeable in your sight to serve the LORD, choose for yourselves today whom you will serve: whether the gods which your fathers served which were beyond the River, or the gods of the Amorites in whose land you are living; but as for me and my house, we will serve the LORD." 16 The people answered and said, "Far be it from us that we should forsake the LORD to serve other gods.

John 8:32 (NIV)
"Then you will know the truth, and the truth will set you free."

My child,

When will you believe me? Why do you doubt my love for you? I know what is best for you but, you continue to take matters into your own hands. Why can't you trust me to work everything for your good? I'm asking you today to stop striving for control, and start abiding in my love for you. You were created by my love, now is the time to abide in my love. Trust me like never before, and you will find peace like you have never known.

I Love You ~♥~

John 14:1-3 (KJV)
Let not your heart be troubled: ye believe in God, believe also in me. In my Father's house are many mansions: if it were not so, I would have told you. I go to prepare a place for you. And if I go and prepare a place for you, I will come again, and receive you unto myself; that where I am, there ye may be also.

Romans 8:28 (KJV)
And we know that all things work together for good to them that love God, to them who are the called according to his purpose.

Psalm 46:10 (NASB)
"Cease striving and know that I am God; I will be exalted among the nations, I will be exalted in the earth."

John 14:27 (ESV)
Peace I leave with you; my peace I give to you. Not as the world gives do I give to you. Let not your hearts be troubled, neither let them be afraid.

My Child,

_____
_____
_____
_____
_____
_____
_____
_____
_____
_____
_____
_____
_____
_____
_____
_____
_____
_____
_____
_____
_____
_____
_____
_____
_____
_____
_____
_____
_____
_____
_____

I Love You

Look to Him not them

My child,

Every day I give you opportunities to follow me - the choice is yours to make. When you're running late and you're joyful instead of anxious - you're choosing to follow me. If in times of financial uncertainties, you remain confident in my word instead of robbing me - you're choosing to follow me. When you open the eyes to your heart, you will see me like never before. I am here with you. Be watchful and choose to follow me.

I Love You ~♥~

Matthew 16:24 (NIV)
Then Jesus said to his disciples, "Whoever wants to be my disciple must deny themselves and take up their cross and follow me.

James 1:2-8 (NIV)
Consider it pure joy, my brothers and sisters, whenever you face trials of many kinds, 3 because you know that the testing of your faith produces perseverance. 4 Let perseverance finish its work so that you may be mature and complete, not lacking anything. 5 If any of you lacks wisdom, you should ask God, who gives generously to all without finding fault, and it will be given to you. 6 But when you ask, you must believe and not doubt, because the one who doubts is like a wave of the sea, blown and tossed by the wind. 7 That person should not expect to receive anything from the Lord. 8 Such a person is double-minded and unstable in all they do.

Malachi 3:8 (NIV)
"Will a mere mortal rob God? Yet you rob me. "But you ask, 'How are we robbing you?' "In tithes and offerings.

My child,

Be bold and courageous for I am with you. Take time to get to know me, and you will understand me better. As you understand me better, I will bring clarity to every situation you are facing. No longer will you hang your head in fear when confronted with a problem, but turn your face up to me. It's time to face the giants in your life, RISE UP in faith and know that I AM in control.

I Love You ~♥~

Philippians 4:6-9 (NIV)
"Do not be anxious about anything, but in everything, by prayer and petition, with thanksgiving, present your requests to God. 7 And the peace of God, which transcends all understanding, will guard your hearts and your minds in Christ Jesus. 8 Finally, brothers, whatever is true, whatever is noble, whatever is right, whatever is pure, whatever is lovely, whatever is admirable--if anything is excellent or praiseworthy--think about such things. 9 Whatever you have learned or received or heard from me, or seen in me--put it into practice. And the God of peace will be with you."

1 Samuel 17:44-46 (ESV)
The Philistine said to David, "Come to me, and I will give your flesh to the birds of the air and to the beasts of the field." 45 Then David said to the Philistine, "You come to me with a sword and with a spear and with a javelin, but I come to you in the name of the Lord of hosts, the God of the armies of Israel, whom you have defied. 46 This day the Lord will deliver you into my hand, and I will strike you down and cut off your head. And I will give the dead bodies of the host of the Philistines this day to the birds of the air and to the wild beasts of the earth, that all the earth may know that there is a God in Israel.

My child,

What is most important in your life? Is it me? Rest assured you are most important to me. Today, I challenge you to reevaluate what is most important to you. Wherever your heart is, there will be your treasure. You are a priceless treasure, loved beyond measure, and created for my pleasure.

I Love You ~♥~

Luke 12:29-31 (NLT)
"And don't be concerned about what to eat and what to drink. Don't worry about such things. 30 These things dominate the thoughts of unbelievers all over the world, but your Father already knows your needs. 31 Seek the Kingdom of God above all else, and he will give you everything you need.

Exodus 20:3 (ISV)
You are to have no other gods as a substitute for me.

Matthew 22:37 (NAS)
And He said to him, " 'YOU SHALL LOVE THE LORD YOUR GOD WITH ALL YOUR HEART, AND WITH ALL YOUR SOUL, AND WITH ALL YOUR MIND.'

Luke 12:34 (ESV)
For where your treasure is, there will your heart be also.

Psalm 103:11-12 (NLT)
For his unfailing love toward those who fear him is as great as the height of the heavens above the earth.

My child,

Time and time again I have shown you my power in your life. Why do you still doubt me? It is my desire for you to be victorious. In fact, I made a way for you to live in Victory! You will be victorious when in your weakness, you fully rely on my strength.

I Love You ~♥~

Jeremiah 10:11-15 (NLT)
Say this to those who worship other gods: "Your so-called gods, who did not make the heavens and earth, will vanish from the earth and from under the heavens." 12 But the Lord made the earth by his power, and he preserves it by his wisdom. With his own understanding he stretched out the heavens. 13 When he speaks in the thunder, the heavens roar with rain. He causes the clouds to rise over the earth. He sends the lightning with the rain and releases the wind from his storehouses. 14 The whole human race is foolish and has no knowledge! The craftsmen are disgraced by the idols they make,for their carefully shaped works are a fraud. These idols have no breath or power. 15 Idols are worthless; they are ridiculous lies! On the day of reckoning they will all be destroyed.

2 Corinthians 12:9-10 (NLT)
Each time he said, "My grace is all you need. My power works best in weakness." So now I am glad to boast about my weaknesses, so that the power of Christ can work through me. 10 That's why I take pleasure in my weaknesses, and in the insults, hardships, persecutions, and troubles that I suffer for Christ. For when I am weak, then I am strong.

My child,

I have a divine order for your life. If you feel pressure, that is coming from trying to perform and please man. If you feel like you're never going to "catch up", you are trying to achieve within your own strength. If you live in chaos and confusion, you are not living in the light of my truth. Today take time with me, ask me what you should be doing. You may be surprised that your ways are not my will for your life. Ask me, and I will answer!

I Love You ~♥~

Proverbs 16:7 (KJV)
When a man's ways please the LORD, he maketh even his enemies to be at peace with him.

Psalm 31:15 (ESV)
My times are in your hand; rescue me from the hand of my enemies and from my persecutors!

3 John 1:4 (NIV)
I have no greater joy than to hear that my children are walking in the truth.

1 John 1:6 (NIV)
If we claim to have fellowship with him and yet walk in the darkness, we lie and do not live out the truth.

Jeremiah 29:11 (NLT)
"For I know the plans I have for you," says the LORD. "They are plans for good and not for disaster, to give you a future and a hope."

My Child,

I Love You

FAITH

IT **till** YOU

make it

My child,

I will meet you each and every time you make yourself available to me. If you feel distant from me, is it I that has moved? No, I remain the same. You will never be abandoned by me. You will feel my presence when you trust me enough with the present and let go of the past.

I Love You ~♥~

Psalm 63: 1-4 (KJV)
O God, thou art my God; early will I seek thee: my soul thirsteth for thee, my flesh longeth for thee in a dry and thirsty land, where no water is; 2 To see thy power and thy glory, so as I have seen thee in the sanctuary. 3 Because thy lovingkindness is better than life, my lips shall praise thee. 4 Thus will I bless thee while I live: I will lift up my hands in thy name.

Deuteronomy 31:5-6 (NASB)
"The LORD will deliver them up before you, and you shall do to them according to all the commandments which I have commanded you. 6"Be strong and courageous, do not be afraid or tremble at them, for the LORD your God is the one who goes with you. He will not fail you or forsake you."

Philippians 3:12-14(ESV)
Not that I have already obtained this or am already perfect, but I press on to make it my own, because Christ Jesus has made me his own. 13 Brothers, I do not consider that I have made it my own. But one thing I do: forgetting what lies behind and straining forward to what lies ahead, 14 I press on toward the goal for the prize of the upward call of God in Christ Jesus.

My child,

I want you to come away from all distractions, and find me in the secret place. I have so much more for you, but it will not be released until you press in and bring your whole heart. I cannot fill a divided heart.

I Love You ~♥~

Psalm 91 : 1-2 (KJV)
He that dwelleth in the secret place of the most High shall abide under the shadow of the Almighty. 2 I will say of the Lord, He is my refuge and my fortress: my God; in him will I trust.

Proverbs 4:23-27 (MSG)
Keep vigilant watch over your heart; that's where life starts. Don't talk out of both sides of your mouth; avoid careless banter, white lies, and gossip. Keep your eyes straight ahead; ignore all sideshow distractions. Watch your step, and the road will stretch out smooth before you. Look neither right nor left; leave evil in the dust.

John 15:8 (NIV)
This is to my Father's glory, that you bear much fruit, showing yourselves to be my disciples.

Colossians 3:2 (KJV)
Set your affection on things above, not on things on the earth.

Matthew 6:24 (AMP)
No one can serve two masters; for either he will hate the one and love the other, or he will stand by and be devoted to the one and despise and be against the other. You cannot serve God and mammon (deceitful riches, money, possessions, or whatever is trusted in).

My child,

Yes, I hear your prayers, yes, I see your situation and yes, I know the dilemma you are facing. That's not even the question. The question is, "Will you believe me to work through these situations and dilemmas you are facing?" Not looking to manmade methods, but looking for me to show you my favor in the midst of uncertain times - will you believe me?

I Love You ~♥~

1 Peter 3:11-13 (NLT)
Turn away from evil and do good. Search for peace, and work to maintain it. 12 The eyes of the Lord watch over those who do right, and his ears are open to their prayers. But the Lord turns his face against those who do evil." 13 Now, who will want to harm you if you are eager to do good?

2 Chronicles 16:9 (ESV)
For the eyes of the Lord run to and fro throughout the whole earth, to give strong support to those whose heart is blameless toward him. You have done foolishly in this, for from now on you will have wars."

Proverbs 3:3-7 (NASB)
Do not let kindness and truth leave you; Bind them around your neck, Write them on the tablet of your heart. 4 So you will find favor and good repute in the sight of God and man. 5 Trust in the Lord with all your heart And do not lean on your own understanding. 6 In all your ways acknowledge Him, And He will make your paths straight. 7 Do not be wise in your own eyes; Fear the Lord and turn away from evil.

John 20:29 (AMP)
Jesus said to him, "Because you have seen Me, do you now believe? Blessed [happy, spiritually secure, and favored by God] are they who did not see [Me] and yet believed [in Me]."

My child,

Do you have a vision for this moment, day, week, month and year? Without a vision you will surely perish. There is a real enemy with a mission to steal, kill and destroy your vision, and ultimately your life. Today, take time and purpose in your heart to discover what your true vision is for the moment, day, week, month and year. There is a work that only you can do, ask me, and I will reveal it to you.

I Love You ~♥~

Proverbs 29:18 (ESV)
Where there is no prophetic vision the people cast off restraint, but blessed is he who keeps the law.

John 10:10 (NIV)
The thief comes only to steal and kill and destroy; I have come that they may have life, and have it to the full.

2 Corinthians 9:7 (KJV)
"Every man according as he purposeth in his heart, so let him give; not grudgingly, or of necessity: for God loveth a cheerful giver."

Ezekiel 12:23 (NIV)
But I the LORD will speak what I will, and it shall be fulfilled without delay. For in your days, you rebellious people, I will fulfill whatever I say, declares the Sovereign LORD.'"

Ephesians 3:20 (NLT)
Now all glory to God, who is able, through his mighty power at work within us, to accomplish infinitely more than we might ask or think

My child,

I am breaking down the protective walls that you have built around your heart. Trust me fully to be your protector. When you isolate yourself and pull in, you render yourself useless for my Kingdom. I've called you to go into the world and take my good news. Resist the fear of man. I am with you, I am mighty to save you. Rise up, march on!

I Love You ~♥~

Joshua 6:1-5 (ESV)
Now Jericho was shut up inside and outside because of the people of Israel. None went out, and none came in. 2 And the Lord said to Joshua, "See, I have given Jericho into your hand, with its king and mighty men of valor. 3 You shall march around the city, all the men of war going around the city once. Thus shall you do for six days. 4 Seven priests shall bear seven trumpets of rams' horns before the ark. On the seventh day you shall march around the city seven times, and the priests shall blow the trumpets. 5 And when they make a long blast with the ram's horn, when you hear the sound of the trumpet, then all the people shall shout with a great shout, and the wall of the city will fall down flat, and the people shall go up, everyone straight before him."

Isaiah 48:17 (NET)
This is what the Lord, your protector, says, the Holy One of Israel: "I am the Lord your God, who teaches you how to succeed, who leads you in the way you should go.

Isaiah 63:1 (NIV)
Who is this coming from Edom, from Bozrah, with his garments stained crimson? Who is this, robed in splendor, striding forward in the greatness of his strength? "It is I, proclaiming victory, mighty to save."

My Child,

I Love You

My child,

You are the apple of my eye, my most prized possession. I love you with an everlasting love and nothing can ever separate you from my love. Today, I invite you to bask in my unfailing love, to receive and believe, I am on your side and working for your good.

I Love You ~♥~

Jeremiah 31:3 (NIV)
The LORD appeared to us in the past, saying: "I have loved you with an
everlasting love; I have drawn you with unfailing kindness."

Romans 8:31-39 (NLT)
What shall we say about such wonderful things as these? If God is for us, who can ever be against us? 32 Since he did not spare even his own Son but gave him up for us all, won't he also give us everything else? 33 Who dares accuse us whom God has chosen for his own? No one—for God himself has given us right standing with himself. 34 Who then will condemn us? No one—for Christ Jesus died for us and was raised to life for us, and he is sitting in the place of honor at God's right hand, pleading for us. 35 Can anything ever separate us from Christ's love? Does it mean he no longer loves us if we have trouble or calamity, or are persecuted, or hungry, or destitute, or in danger, or threatened with death? 36 As the Scriptures say, "For your sake we are killed every day; we are being slaughtered like sheep." 37 No, despite all these things, overwhelming victory is ours through Christ, who loved us. 38 And I am convinced that nothing can ever separate us from God's love. Neither death nor life, neither angels nor demons, neither our fears for today nor our worries about tomorrow—not even the powers of hell can separate us from God's love. 39 No power in the sky above or in the earth below—indeed, nothing in all creation will ever be able to separate us from the love of God that is revealed in Christ Jesus our Lord.

My child,

I know you feel troubled and pressed on every side. You search for peace and safety, but there is none to be found in this world. Remember this place is not your home, you are just passing through. I am with you as you endure trials and temptations. Look to me, I will show you the way to escape the trappings of this world.

I Love You ~♥~

2 Corinthians 4:8-12 (NLT)
We are pressed on every side by troubles, but we are not crushed. We are perplexed, but not driven to despair. 9 We are hunted down, but never abandoned by God. We get knocked down, but we are not destroyed. 10 Through suffering, our bodies continue to share in the death of Jesus so that the life of Jesus may also be seen in our bodies .11 Yes, we live under constant danger of death because we serve Jesus, so that the life of Jesus will be evident in our dying bodies. 12 So we live in the face of death, but this has resulted in eternal life for you.

Hebrews 13:14 (NLT)
For this world is not our permanent home; we are looking forward to a home yet to come.

1 Corinthians 10:13 (ESV)
No temptation has overtaken you that is not common to man. God is faithful, and he will not let you be tempted beyond your ability, but with the temptation he will also provide the way of escape, that you may be able to endure it.

My child,

The past several months you have faced many mountains and valleys. With every high and every low, I am with you. Through this time of testing, your spiritual discernment has grown deeper and your eyes have seen the deceptive workings of the enemy. Draw closer to me, stand firm in faith and allow me to bring victory to your life.

I Love You ~♥~

Isaiah 40:3-5 (ESV)
A voice cries: "In the wilderness prepare the way of the Lord; make straight in the desert a highway for our God. 4 Every valley shall be lifted up, and every mountain and hill be made low; the uneven ground shall become level, and the rough places a plain. 5 And the glory of the Lord shall be revealed, and all flesh shall see it together, for the mouth of the Lord has spoken."

2 Timothy 3:12-13 (NIV)
In fact, everyone who wants to live a godly life in Christ Jesus will be persecuted, 13 while evildoers and impostors will go from bad to worse, deceiving and being deceived.

2 Chronicles 20:17 (NIV)
"You will not have to fight this battle. Take up your positions; stand firm and see the deliverance the LORD will give you, Judah and Jerusalem. Do not be afraid; do not be discouraged. Go out to face them tomorrow, and the LORD will be with you.'"

1 Corinthians 15:57 (NIV)
But thanks be to God! He gives us the victory through our Lord Jesus Christ

My child,

When will you realize I am all you need? You must stop striving to find the answers. If you could solve the puzzle of life, then where would faith abide? This life is one of faith and not of sight. Believe me and you will see me. When you place me first, all the other pieces will perfectly fit together.

I Love You ~♥~

John 14:6 (NIV)
Jesus answered, "I am the way and the truth and the life. No one comes to the Father except through me.

2 Peter 1:3 (NLT)
By his divine power, God has given us everything we need for living a godly life. We have received all of this by coming to know him, the one who called us to himself by means of his marvelous glory and excellence.

My child,

You can know the joy of eternity on earth, as you walk with great expectation and excitement of your heavenly home. The joy of eternity is contagious. Others will notice your freedom and desire what you have. As you share joy with others, you are sharing me.

I Love You ~♥~

Psalm 51:12-16 (NLT)
Restore to me the joy of your salvation, and make me willing to obey you. 13 Then I will teach your ways to rebels, and they will return to you. 14 Forgive me for shedding blood, O God who saves; then I will joyfully sing of your forgiveness. 15 Unseal my lips, O Lord, that my mouth may praise you.

2 Corinthians 4:18 (NLT)
So we don't look at the troubles we can see now; rather, we fix our gaze on things that cannot be seen. For the things we see now will soon be gone, but the things we cannot see will last forever.

Proverbs 3:5-12 (MSG)
Trust God from the bottom of your heart; don't try to figure out everything on your own. Listen for God's voice in everything you do, everywhere you go; he's the one who will keep you on track. Don't assume that you know it all. Run to God! Run from evil! Your body will glow with health, your very bones will vibrate with life! Honor God with everything you own; give him the first and the best. Your barns will burst, your wine vats will brim over. But don't, dear friend, resent God's discipline; don't sulk under his loving correction. It's the child he loves that God corrects; a father's delight is behind all this.

My Child,

_____
_____
_____
_____
_____
_____
_____
_____
_____
_____
_____
_____
_____
_____
_____
_____
_____
_____
_____
_____
_____
_____
_____
_____
_____
_____
_____
_____

I Love You

~~

THE Anointing IS NEVER disappointing

My child,

You are everything I created you to be. It was I that formed you in the womb giving you all your special abilities and qualities. I want you today to step into your divine destiny with me, walking in the spirit and not the flesh. Embrace who you are in me and love what I've created in you.

I Love you ~♥~

Ephesians 2:7-10 (MSG)
Now God has us where he wants us, with all the time in this world and the next to shower grace and kindness upon us in Christ Jesus. Saving is all his idea, and all his work. All we do is trust him enough to let him do it. It's God's gift from start to finish! We don't play the major role. If we did, we'd probably go around bragging that we'd done the whole thing! No, we neither make nor save ourselves. God does both the making and saving. He creates each of us by Christ Jesus to join him in the work he does, the good work he has gotten ready for us to do, work we had better be doing.

1 Peter 4:10-11 (NLT)
God has given each of you a gift from his great variety of spiritual gifts. Use them well to serve one another. 11 Do you have the gift of speaking? Then speak as though God himself were speaking through you. Do you have the gift of helping others? Do it with all the strength and energy that God supplies. Then everything you do will bring glory to God through Jesus Christ. All glory and power to him forever and ever! Amen.

Galatians 5:16 (NLT)
So I say, let the Holy Spirit guide your lives. Then you won't be doing what your sinful nature craves.

My child,

It is time for you to allow me to prune away the dead branches from your heart. Dead branches are attachments that drain the life out of you. Pruning prepares you for new growth, and healthy branches will produce good fruit. Attach yourself to me, I am your life giving source.

I Love you ~♥~

Luke 13:6-7 (NLT)
Then Jesus told this story: "A man planted a fig tree in his garden and came again and again to see if there was any fruit on it, but he was always disappointed. 7 Finally, he said to his gardener, 'I've waited three years, and there hasn't been a single fig! Cut it down. It's just taking up space in the garden.'

John 15:1-5 (NLT)
"I am the true grapevine, and my Father is the gardener. 2 He cuts off every branch of mine that doesn't produce fruit, and he prunes the branches that do bear fruit so they will produce even more. 3 You have already been pruned and purified by the message I have given you. 4 Remain in me, and I will remain in you. For a branch cannot produce fruit if it is severed from the vine, and you cannot be fruitful unless you remain in me. 5 "Yes, I am the vine; you are the branches. Those who remain in me, and I in them, will produce much fruit. For apart from me you can do nothing.

Psalm 1:1-3 (ESV)
Blessed is the man who walks not in the counsel of the wicked, nor stands in the way of sinners, nor sits in the seat of scoffers; 2 but his delight is in the law of the Lord, and on his law he meditates day and night. 3 He is like a tree planted by streams of water that yields its fruit in its season, and its leaf does not wither. In all that he does, he prospers.

My child,

You have been faithful to follow me even when it did not make sense. Your obedience will be rewarded, because I am the rewarder of those who diligently seek and obey me. My ways are higher; thank you for taking the high road with me.

I Love You ~♥~

Matthew 16:24 (NIV)
"Then said Jesus unto his disciples, If any man will come after me, let him deny himself, and take up his cross, and follow me." (KJV)

John 8:12 (NIV)
"When Jesus spoke again to the people, he said, "I am the light of the world. Whoever follows me will never walk in darkness, but will have the light of life."

Hebrews 11:6 (KJV)
But without faith it is impossible to please him: for he that cometh to God must believe that he is, and that he is a rewarder of them that diligently seek him

Isaiah 55:8-9 (NIV)
"For my thoughts are not your thoughts, neither are your ways my ways," declares the Lord. 9 "As the heavens are higher than the earth, so are my ways higher than your ways and my thoughts than your thoughts.

My child,

The time has come for you to rise up in the authority I have given to you. There is no room for fear in the heart of a warrior. You must have reckless abandonment to me and place your trust in me with all your heart. I will protect and guide you to victory! Do not fear what is ahead of you. I am near!

I Love you ~♥~

2 Corinthians 9:6-15 (MSG)
Remember: A stingy planter gets a stingy crop; a lavish planter gets a lavish crop. I want each of you to take plenty of time to think it over, and make up your own mind what you will give. That will protect you against sob stories and arm-twisting. God loves it when the giver delights in the giving. 8-11 God can pour on the blessings in astonishing ways so that you're ready for anything and everything, more than just ready to do what needs to be done. As one psalmist puts it, He throws caution to the winds, giving to the needy in reckless abandon. His right-living, right-giving ways never run out, never wear out. This most generous God who gives seed to the farmer that becomes bread for your meals is more than extravagant with you. He gives you something you can then give away, which grows into full-formed lives, robust in God, wealthy in every way, so that you can be generous in every way, producing with us great praise to God. 12-15 Carrying out this social relief work involves far more than helping meet the bare needs of poor Christians. It also produces abundant and bountiful thanksgivings to God. This relief offering is a prod to live at your very best, showing your gratitude to God by being openly obedient to the plain meaning of the Message of Christ.

My child,

You are struggling with many unnecessary things that are weighing you down. If you will surrender those areas to me, I will make an exchange with you and give you my peace. You have two choices - keep your problems or receive my peace. The choice is yours to make. Choose you this day who you will serve.

I Love you ~♥~

Hebrews 12:1-3 (NLT)
Therefore, since we are surrounded by such a huge crowd of witnesses to the life of faith, let us strip off every weight that slows us down, especially the sin that so easily trips us up. And let us run with endurance the race God has set before us. 2 We do this by keeping our eyes on Jesus, the champion who initiates and perfects our faith. Because of the joy awaiting him, he endured the cross, disregarding its shame. Now he is seated in the place of honor beside God's throne. 3 Think of all the hostility he endured from sinful people; then you won't become weary and give up.

Philippians 4:6-7 (NLT)
Don't worry about anything; instead, pray about everything. Tell God what you need, and thank him for all he has done. 7 Then you will experience God's peace, which exceeds anything we can understand. His peace will guard your hearts and minds as you live in Christ Jesus.

J
oshua 24:15 (KJV)
And if it seem evil unto you to serve the LORD, choose you this day whom ye will serve; whether the gods which your fathers served that were on the other side of the flood, or the gods of the Amorites, in whose land ye dwell: but as for me and my house, we will serve the LORD.

My Child,

_____

_____

_____

_____

_____

_____

_____

_____

_____

_____

_____

_____

_____

_____

_____

_____

_____

_____

_____

_____

_____

_____

_____

_____

_____

_____

_____

_____

_____

_____

I Love You

~ ~

My child,

Before the beginning of time, I knew you. I've had a plan for your life even before you were formed in the womb. And to this day, I know how many hairs are on your head. I am a God of details. You never have to doubt me or my plans for you. Let go of the fear and follow me. I will never lead you astray.

I Love You ~♥~

Ephesians 1:4-5 (NLT)
Even before he made the world, God loved us and chose us in Christ to be holy and without fault in his eyes. 5 God decided in advance to adopt us into his own family by bringing us to himself through Jesus Christ. This is what he wanted to do, and it gave him great pleasure.

Matthew 10:29-31 (MSG)
"What's the price of a pet canary? Some loose change, right? And God cares what happens to it even more than you do. He pays even greater attention to you, down to the last detail—even numbering the hairs on your head! So don't be intimidated by all this bully talk. You're worth more than a million canaries.

John 10:27-29 (NLT)
My sheep listen to my voice; I know them, and they follow me. 28 I give them eternal life, and they will never perish. No one can snatch them away from me, 29 for my Father has given them to me, and he is more powerful than anyone else. No one can snatch them from the Father's hand.

My child,

There have been times you thought, this is impossible, I can't do this, or I'm not good enough. I am here in this moment to reaffirm you and say to you this day - What you call impossible, I say is possible! What you say can't be done, I say yes, it can! When you say you're not good enough, I say you are more than enough! Never lose sight of my power working through your life. I Love you ~♥~

Mark 10:27 (NIV)
Jesus looked at them and said, "With man this is impossible, but not with God; all things are possible with God."

Philippians 2:12-15 (NLT)
Dear friends, you always followed my instructions when I was with you. And now that I am away, it is even more important. Work hard to show the results of your salvation, obeying God with deep reverence and fear. 13 For God is working in you, giving you the desire and the power to do what pleases him. 14 Do everything without complaining and arguing, 15 so that no one can criticize you. Live clean, innocent lives as children of God, shining like bright lights in a world full of crooked and perverse people.

James 1:17 (NLT)
Whatever is good and perfect comes down to us from God our Father, who created all the lights in the heavens. He never changes or casts a shifting shadow.

Ephesians 3:20 (NIV)
Now to him who is able to do immeasurably more than all we ask or imagine, according to his power that is at work within us.

My child,

When you drop your defensiveness I can bless your life. When you are self-protecting, you are not fully trusting me. I am your protector, trust me with all your heart. Lower your shield of self-protection and allow me full access to your life.

I Love You ~♥~

2 Thessalonians 3:3 (AMP)
But the Lord is faithful, and He will strengthen you [setting you on a firm foundation] and will protect and guard you from the evil one.

Deuteronomy 31:6 (ESV)
"Be strong and courageous. Do not fear or be in dread of them, for it is the Lord your God who goes with you. He will not leave you or forsake you."

Psalm 34:19 (HCSB)
Many adversities come to the one who is righteous, but the Lord delivers him from them all.

Psalm 138:7 (KJV)
Though I walk in the midst of trouble, thou wilt revive me: thou shalt stretch forth thine hand against the wrath of mine enemies, and thy right hand shall save me.

1 Thessalonians 5:23-24 (MSG)
May God himself, the God who makes everything holy and whole, make you holy and whole, put you together—spirit, soul, and body—and keep you fit for the coming of our Master, Jesus Christ. The One who called you is completely dependable. If he said it, he'll do it!

My child,

I will always fight for you. When you experience times of disappointments, it isn't that I've not heard your prayers. Reexamine your heart motives and expectations. There you will find the source of your disappointments. When things don't go as planned, trust me for a greater outcome. I will never disappoint you.

I Love You ~♥~

Exodus 14:14 (ESV)
"The LORD will fight for you, and you have only to be silent."

James 4:3 (NIV)
When you ask, you do not receive, because you ask with wrong motives,
that you may spend what you get on your pleasures.

Proverbs 16:3 (NIV)
Commit to the Lord whatever you do, and he will establish your plans.

Romans 5:5 (NLT)
And this hope will not lead to disappointment. For we know how dearly God loves us, because he has given us the Holy Spirit to fill our hearts with his love

My child,

I do not ask you to bear your burdens. When you feel the weight of life's issues, it is because you are lacking faith and put your trust in other places apart from me. Cast your burdens on me and trust that I will carry them for you. When you release them, peace will abide within your heart.

I Love You ~♥~

Psalm 68:19-20 (NIV)
The Lord deserves praise! Day after day he carries our burden, the God who delivers us. Our God is a God who delivers; the LORD, the sovereign Lord, can rescue from death.

Matthew 11:29-30 (NIV)
Take my yoke upon you. Let me teach you, because I am humble and gentle at heart, and you will find rest for your souls. 30 For my yoke is easy to bear, and the burden I give you is light.

Psalm 138:7 (ESV)
Though I walk in the midst of trouble, you preserve my life; you stretch out your hand against the wrath of my enemies, and your right hand delivers me.

Psalm 55:22 (NIV)
Cast your cares on the LORD and he will sustain you; he will never let the righteous be shaken.

John 14:27 (NLT)
"I am leaving you with a gift--peace of mind and heart. And the peace I give is a gift the world cannot give. So don't be troubled or afraid.

My Child,

I Love You

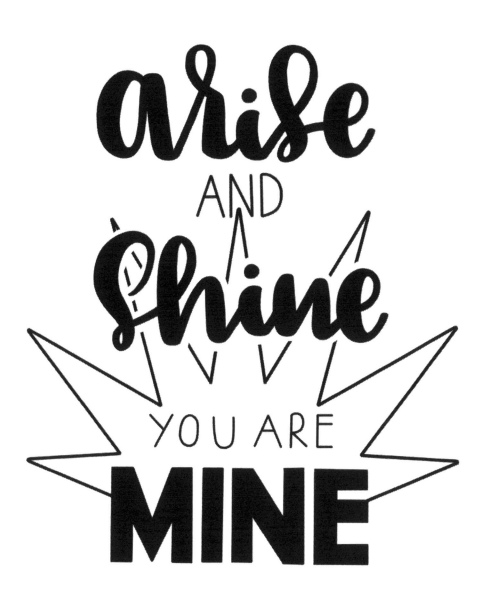

My child,

I want to reaffirm to you that man's rejection is my protection. When you seek others first for fulfillment or validation, you will be disappointed. I am the true source of fulfillment. In me lies no deception, I will always guide you in the truth. Run to me with all your heart, I will give you complete fulfillment and my unwavering protection. I Love You ~♥~

Romans 3:2-6 (MSG)
First, there's the matter of being put in charge of writing down and caring for God's revelation, these Holy Scriptures. So, what if, in the course of doing that, some of those Jews abandoned their post? God didn't abandon them. Do you think their faithlessness cancels out his faithfulness? Not on your life! Depend on it: God keeps his word even when the whole world is lying through its teeth. Scripture says the same: Your words stand fast and true; Rejection doesn't faze you. But if our wrongdoing only underlines and confirms God's rightdoing, shouldn't we be commended for helping out? Since our bad words don't even make a dent in his good words, isn't it wrong of God to back us to the wall and hold us to our word? These questions come up. The answer to such questions is no, a most emphatic No! How else would things ever get straightened out if God didn't do the straightening?

Philippians 1:10-11 (NASB)
So that you may approve the things that are excellent, in order to be sincere and blameless until the day of Christ; having been filled with the fruit of righteousness which comes through Jesus Christ, to the glory and praise of God.

2 Corinthians 4:2 (NLT)
We reject all shameful deeds and underhanded methods. We don't try to trick anyone or distort the word of God. We tell the truth before God, and all who are honest know this.

My child,

Today I want you to be my tangible love. There are so many wounded people that feel undeserving of my love. You can show them my love by your actions. Hold them with a hug, share a smile, speak sweet words or love with laughter. Put my love into action! I Love You ~♥~

Luke 10:33-35(NLT)
"Then a despised Samaritan came along, and when he saw the man, he felt compassion for him. 34 Going over to him, the Samaritan soothed his wounds with olive oil and wine and bandaged them. Then he put the man on his own donkey and took him to an inn, where he took care of him. 35 The next day he handed the innkeeper two silver coins, telling him, 'Take care of this man. If his bill runs higher than this, I'll pay you the next time I'm here.

Romans 12:9-21 (MSG)
Love from the center of who you are; don't fake it. Run for dear life from evil; hold on for dear life to good. Be good friends who love deeply; practice playing second fiddle. 11-13 Don't burn out; keep yourselves fueled and aflame. Be alert servants of the Master, cheerfully expectant. Don't quit in hard times; pray all the harder. Help needy Christians; be inventive in hospitality. 14-16 Bless your enemies; no cursing under your breath. Laugh with your happy friends when they're happy; share tears when they're down. Get along with each other; don't be stuck-up. Make friends with nobodies; don't be the great somebody. 17-19 Don't hit back; discover beauty in everyone. If you've got it in you, get along with everybody. Don't insist on getting even; that's not for you to do. "I'll do the judging," says God. "I'll take care of it." 20-21 Our Scriptures tell us that if you see your enemy hungry, go buy that person lunch, or if he's thirsty, get him a drink. Your generosity will surprise him with goodness. Don't let evil get the best of you; get the best of evil by doing good.

My child,

I ask of you to give me more time. I will give you the strength you need to complete every task at hand, but first things first. I must be first. You will find increase of time when you give me the first fruits of each and every day. Seek me first and I will arrange your day. Adding more of me will ensure the increase you desire!

I Love you ~♥~

Proverbs 3:1-2 (ESV)
My son, do not forget my teaching, but let your heart keep my commandments, 2 for length of days and years of life and peace they will add to you.

2 Chronicles 31:21 (ESV)
And every work that he undertook in the service of the house of God and in accordance with the law and the commandments, seeking his God, he did with all his heart, and prospered.

Psalm 31:14-17 (MSG)
Desperate, I throw myself on you: you are my God! Hour by hour I place my days in your hand, safe from the hands out to get me. Warm me, your servant, with a smile; save me because you love me. Don't embarrass me by not showing up; I've given you plenty of notice.

Matthew 6:33 (KJV)
But seek ye first the kingdom of God, and his righteousness; and all these things shall be added unto you.

My child,

The days ahead of you are most important. How you respond and react in certain situations will determine the duration. I see your heart and the areas that do not fully belong to me. Until you fully trust me, you will find yourself facing situations that require you to fully surrender your whole heart. You can trust me.

I Love You ~♥~

1 Peter 4:12-13 (NLT)
Dear friends, don't be surprised at the fiery trials you are going through, as if something strange were happening to you. 13 Instead, be very glad—for these trials make you partners with Christ in his suffering, so that you will have the wonderful joy of seeing his glory when it is revealed to all the world.

Galatians 6:8-10 (NLT)
8 Those who live only to satisfy their own sinful nature will harvest decay and death from that sinful nature. But those who live to please the Spirit will harvest everlasting life from the Spirit. 9 So let's not get tired of doing what is good. At just the right time we will reap a harvest of blessing if we don't give up. 10 Therefore, whenever we have the opportunity, we should do good to everyone—especially to those in the family of faith.

1 Kings 8:61 (KJV)
Let your heart therefore be wholly true to the Lord our God, walking in his statutes and keeping his commandments, as at this day."

Jeremiah 17:10 (KJV)
"I the Lord search the heart and test the mind, to give every man according to his ways, according to the fruit of his deeds."

My child,

I am strong in your weakness. Why do you worry about being dependent on me? Total dependency is what I want from you. The world's view is independence from me, don't fall into that trap. By allowing me to be Lord over your life, I am given opportunities to show my power through your life.

I Love you ~♥~

Psalm 62:5-12 (KJV)
My soul, wait thou only upon God; for my expectation is from him. He only is my rock and my salvation: he is my defence; I shall not be moved. In God is my salvation and my glory: the rock of my strength, and my refuge, is in God. Trust in him at all times; ye people, pour out your heart before him: God is a refuge for us. Selah. Surely men of low degree are vanity, and men of high degree are a lie: to be laid in the balance, they are altogether lighter than vanity. Trust not in oppression, and become not vain in robbery: if riches increase, set not your heart upon them. God hath spoken once; twice have I heard this; that power belongeth unto God. Also unto thee, O Lord, belongeth mercy: for thou renderest to every man according to his work.

2 Corinthians 12:8-10 (NLT)
Three different times I begged the Lord to take it away. Each time he said, "My grace is all you need. My power works best in weakness." So now I am glad to boast about my weaknesses, so that the power of Christ can work through me.That's why I take pleasure in my weaknesses, and in the insults, hardships, persecutions, and troubles that I suffer for Christ. For when I am weak, then I am strong.

My Child,

I Love You

mornings are full of His glories

My child,

My word will never fail you. Unbelief is a barrier that even I cannot cross. Remove all doubt and unbelief from your heart and replace it with complete trust in me. I will not disappoint you. For if you would only believe all things are possible through me; the bondage of unbelief would break in your life.

I Love You ~♥~

Isaiah 55:11 (KJV)
So shall my word be that goeth forth out of my mouth: it shall not return unto me void, but it shall accomplish that which I please, and it shall prosper in the thing whereto I sent it.

Hebrews 3:12-19 (ESV)
Take care, brothers, lest there be in any of you an evil, unbelieving heart, leading you to fall away from the living God. 13 But exhort one another every day, as long as it is called "today," that none of you may be hardened by the deceitfulness of sin. 14 For we have come to share in Christ, if indeed we hold our original confidence firm to the end. 15 As it is said, "Today, if you hear his voice, do not harden your hearts as in the rebellion." 16 For who were those who heard and yet rebelled? Was it not all those who left Egypt led by Moses? 17 And with whom was he provoked for forty years? Was it not with those who sinned, whose bodies fell in the wilderness? 18 And to whom did he swear that they would not enter his rest, but to those who were disobedient? 19 So we see that they were unable to enter because of unbelief.

Matthew 19:26 (NLT)
Jesus looked at them intently and said, "Humanly speaking, it is impossible. But with God everything is possible."

My child,

I do love you! With my love comes discipline. I am not trying to hurt you, but to teach you and make you stronger through my discipline. There is a greater reward for you when you surrender in obedience to me and only follow me.

I Love you ~♥~

Revelation 3:19 (ESV)
Those whom I love, I reprove and discipline, so be zealous and repent.

Hebrews 12:5-6 (NLT)
And have you forgotten the encouraging words God spoke to you as his children? He said,"My child, don't make light of the Lord's discipline and don't give up when he corrects you. 6 For the Lord disciplines those he loves, and he punishes each one he accepts as his child.

Philippians 3:13-15 (NLT)
No, dear brothers and sisters, I have not achieved it, but I focus on this one thing: Forgetting the past and looking forward to what lies ahead, 14 I press on to reach the end of the race and receive the heavenly prize for which God, through Christ Jesus, is calling us. 15 Let all who are spiritually mature agree on these things. If you disagree on some point, I believe God will make it plain to you.

My child,

In order to know my voice you must spend time with me and silence all other voices in your life. If you want to know my will, just ask me and listen for my answer. You can become double minded when you have too many voices speaking at one time. Find a quiet place, seek me and I will meet with you. Call to me, and I will answer you.

I Love you ~♥~

John 10:27-29 (ESV)
My sheep hear my voice, and I know them, and they follow me. 28 I give them eternal life, and they will never perish, and no one will snatch them out of my hand. 29 My Father, who has given them to me, is greater than all, and no one is able to snatch them out of the Father's hand.

James 1:6-9 (NIV)
But when you ask, you must believe and not doubt, because the one who doubts is like a wave of the sea, blown and tossed by the wind. 7 That person should not expect to receive anything from the Lord. 8 Such a person is double-minded and unstable in all they do. 9 Believers in humble circumstances ought to take pride in their high position.

Proverbs 2:1-5 (ESV)
My son, if you receive my words and treasure up my commandments with you, 2 making your ear attentive to wisdom and inclining your heart to understanding; 3 yes, if you call out for insight and raise your voice for understanding, 4 if you seek it like silver and search for it as for hidden treasures, 5 then you will understand the fear of the Lord and find the knowledge of God.

My child,

I will break the bondage in your life. First, you must realize that you have the bondage, renounce it from your life and resist the temptation to go back. You can be free. I am the way to freedom. When I set you free, you are free indeed!

I Love You ~♥~

Acts 8:22-23 Bible (NASB)
Therefore repent of this wickedness of yours, and pray the Lord that, if possible, the intention of your heart may be forgiven you. 23 For I see that you are in the gall of bitterness and in the bondage of iniquity."

2 Timothy 2:22-26 (MSG)
Run away from infantile indulgence. Run after mature righteousness - faith, love, peace - joining those who are in honest and serious prayer before God. Refuse to get involved in inane discussions; they always end up in fights. God's servant must not be argumentative, but a gentle listener and a teacher who keeps cool, working firmly but patiently with those who refuse to obey. You never know how or when God might sober them up with a change of heart and a turning to the truth, enabling them to escape the Devil's trap, where they are caught and held captive, forced to run his errands.

John 14:6 (KJV)
Jesus saith unto him, I am the way, the truth, and the life: no man cometh unto the Father, but by me.

My child,

When you abide in my anointing, everything flows together. If you find yourself frustrated and striving - stop and ask for directions. Even when the path looks good and inviting, you must direct your attention to me for confirmation before you step out. Make sure I am calling you before you answer yes!

I Love You ~♥~

John 15:7(NKJV)
If you abide in Me, and My words abide in you, you will ask what you desire, and it shall be done for you.

Psalm 86:11 (NASB)
Teach me Your way, O LORD; I will walk in Your truth; Unite my heart to fear Your name.

Psalm 143:8 (NASB)
Let me hear Your lovingkindness in the morning; For I trust in You; Teach me the way in which I should walk; For to You I lift up my soul.

Psalm 43:3 (NASB)
O send out Your light and Your truth, let them lead me; Let them bring me to Your holy hill and to Your dwelling places.

Psalm 73:23-24 (NASB)
Nevertheless I am continually with You; You have taken hold of my right hand. With Your counsel You will guide me, And afterward receive me to glory.

Psalm 119:35 (NASB)
Make me walk in the path of Your commandments, For I delight in it.

My Child,

_____

_____

_____

_____

_____

_____

_____

_____

_____

_____

_____

_____

_____

_____

_____

_____

_____

_____

_____

_____

_____

_____

_____

_____

_____

_____

_____

_____

I Love You

~♥~

in spite of that you can do this

My child,

If you only could believe what I have planned for you is good, there would be no room for doubt or worry. You are asking for doors to open for you, but what you may not realize is faith is the key that unlocks the door. You do not have to make anything happen in your life. You only have to believe my words, trust my heart and never doubt my love. I will take care of you. Without faith, it is impossible to please me.

I Love You ~♥~

Jeremiah 29:11-13 (ESV)
For I know the plans I have for you, declares the Lord, plans for welfare and not for evil, to give you a future and a hope. 12 Then you will call upon me and come and pray to me, and I will hear you. 13 You will seek me and find me, when you seek me with all your heart.

Philippians 4:18-20 (MSG)
And now I have it all—and keep getting more! The gifts you sent with Epaphroditus were more than enough, like a sweet-smelling sacrifice roasting on the altar, filling the air with fragrance, pleasing God no end. You can be sure that God will take care of everything you need, his generosity exceeding even yours in the glory that pours from Jesus. Our God and Father abounds in glory that just pours out into eternity. Yes.

Hebrews 11:5-6 (MSG)
By an act of faith, Enoch skipped death completely. "They looked all over and couldn't find him because God had taken him." We know on the basis of reliable testimony that before he was taken "he pleased God." It's impossible to please God apart from faith. And why? Because anyone who wants to approach God must believe both that he exists and that he cares enough to respond to those who seek him.

My child,

Walking with me requires complete trust. You must not look away or lend your affections to other things. With me being first walking in front of you, the path will always be clear. Let me guide you along the path that I have chosen.

I Love You ~♥~

Psalm 25:3-5 (ESV)
Indeed, none who wait for you shall be put to shame; they shall be ashamed who are wantonly treacherous. 4 Make me to know your ways, O Lord; teach me your paths. 5 Lead me in your truth and teach me, for you are the God of my salvation; for you I wait all the day long.

Colossians 3:-2 (MSG)
So if you're serious about living this new resurrection life with Christ, act like it. Pursue the things over which Christ presides. Don't shuffle along, eyes to the ground, absorbed with the things right in front of you. Look up, and be alert to what is going on around Christ—that's where the action is. See things from his perspective.

John 16:13 (AMP)
But when He, the Spirit of Truth, comes, He will guide you into all the truth [full and complete truth]. For He will not speak on His own initiative, but He will speak whatever He hears [from the Father—the message regarding the Son], and He will disclose to you what is to come [in the future].

My child,

I sing over you with songs of love. The melody of my heart is always in tune with your life. I keep perfect time with every rhythm and rhyme. Even when you're playing off key, I keep perfect harmony as I sing over you. Listen closely, tune your ears so that you may hear and sing the song with me.

I Love you ~♥~

Zephaniah 3:16-17 (NLT)
On that day the announcement to Jerusalem will be, "Cheer up, Zion! Don't be afraid! 17 For the Lord your God is living among you. He is a mighty savior. He will take delight in you with gladness. With his love, he will calm all your fears. He will rejoice over you with joyful songs."

Colossians 3:13-14 (ESV)
...bearing with one another and, if one has a complaint against another, forgiving each other; as the Lord has forgiven you, so you also must forgive. 14 And above all these put on love, which binds everything together in perfect harmony.

Proverbs 4:20-22 (MSG)
Dear friend, listen well to my words; tune your ears to my voice. Keep my message in plain view at all times. Concentrate! Learn it by heart! Those who discover these words live, really live; body and soul, they're bursting with health.

My child,

For years now you have wandered around aimlessly without true Kingdom purpose. You must stay at my feet and connected to the true source of your purpose. I have a plan and you have purpose. Come sit in my presence and I will reveal your divine Kingdom purpose.

I Love You ~♥~

Exodus 9:16 (ESV)
But for this purpose I have raised you up, to show you my power, so that my name may be proclaimed in all the earth.

Proverbs 19:21 (MSG)
We humans keep brainstorming options and plans, but God's purpose prevails.

Romans 8:28 (KJV)
And we know that in all things God works for the good of those who love him, who have been called according to his purpose.

My child,

Do not fear. It robs you of joy, peace and rest. I know your situations and circumstances, so do not fear! I call you to walk by faith and not by sight. Look to me and your vision will be changed and you will have a Kingdom perspective.

I Love You ~♥~

Proverbs 12:25 (MSG)
Worry weighs us down; cheerful word picks us up.

Exodus 14:13-14 (NLT)
But Moses told the people, "Don't be afraid. Just stand still and watch the you today. The Egyptians you see today will never be seen again. 14 The Lord himself will fight for you. Just stay calm."

2 Corinthians 5:6-7 (KJV)
Therefore we are always confident, knowing that, whilst we are at home in the body, we are absent from the Lord: 7 For we walk by faith, not by sight.

My Child,

_____
_____
_____
_____
_____
_____
_____
_____
_____
_____
_____
_____
_____
_____
_____
_____
_____
_____
_____
_____
_____
_____
_____
_____
_____
_____
_____
_____
_____
_____
_____

I Love You

savor the favor

My child,

Worship me in Spirit and truth. It's time for the true worshippers to arise. Your worship breaks bondages off your life and stops the enemy's torment. Worship wins over every struggle you are facing. I am worthy of your worship and I am the one that puts passion in your praise.

I Love You ~♥~

John 4:23-24 (KJV)
But the hour cometh, and now is, when the true worshippers shall worship the Father in spirit and in truth: for the Father seeketh such to worship him. 24 God is a Spirit: and they that worship him must worship him in spirit and in truth.

II Chronicles 20:20-24 (NLT)
Early the next morning the army of Judah went out into the wilderness of Tekoa. On the way Jehoshaphat stopped and said, "Listen to me, all you people of Judah and Jerusalem! Believe in the Lord God, and you will be able to stand firm. Believe in his prophets, and you will succeed." After consulting the people, the king appointed singers to walk ahead of the army, singing to the praising him for his holy splendor. This is what they sang: "Give thanks to the; faithful love endures forever!" 22At the very moment they began to sing and give praise, the Lord caused the armies of Ammon, Moab, and Mount Seir to start fighting among themselves. 23The armies of Moab and Ammon turned against their allies from Mount Seir and killed every one of them. After they had destroyed the army of Seir, they began attacking each other. 24So when the army of Judah arrived at the lookout point in the wilderness, all they saw were dead bodies lying on the ground as far as they could see. Not a single one of the enemy had escaped.

Psalm 145:3 (NLT)
Great is the LORD! He is most worthy of praise! No one can measure his greatness.

My child,

I am the way to restoration in your life. You cannot earn my freedom, love or favor. I gave and continue to give it freely to you. I am the great I AM, and because you have chosen to follow me, you can be all that I've called you to be. Your part is only believe and receive!

I Love You ~♥~

Jeremiah 30:17 (ESV)
For I will restore health to you, and your wounds I will heal, declares the Lord.

Isaiah 61:7 (ESV)
Instead of your shame there shall be a double portion; instead of dishonor they shall rejoice in their lot; therefore in their land they shall possess a double portion; they shall have everlasting joy.

Joel 2:25-26 (ESV)
I will restore to you the years that the swarming locust has eaten, the hopper, the destroyer, and the cutter, my great army, which I sent among you. You shall eat in plenty and be satisfied, and praise the name of the Lord your God, who has dealt wondrously with you. And my people shall never again be put to shame.

Isaiah 1:18 (ESV)
Come now, let us reason together, says the LORD: though your sins are like scarlet, they shall be as white as snow; though they are red like crimson, they shall become like wool.

2 Corinthians 5:17 (ESV)
Therefore, if anyone is in Christ, he is a new creation. The old has passed away; behold, the new has come.

My child,

I will reveal things to you and uncover all that is hidden. Trust me and wait. Do not allow your mind to fixate or fabricate. I am in control, let it go, allow me to do my work and have my will be done.

I Love You ~♥~

Daniel 2:21-23 (ESV)
"He changes times and seasons; he removes kings and sets up kings; he gives wisdom to the wise and knowledge to those who have understanding; 22 he reveals deep and hidden things; he knows what is in the darkness, and the light dwells with him. 23 To you, O God of my fathers, I give thanks and praise, for you have given me wisdom and might, and have now made known to me what we asked of you, for you have made known to us the king's matter."

Colossians 3:2 (AMP)
Set your mind and keep focused habitually on the things above [the heavenly things], not on things that are on the earth [which have only temporal value].

Romans 12:2 (KJV)
"And be not conformed to this world: but be ye transformed by the renewing of your mind, that ye may prove what is that good, and acceptable, and perfect, will of God."

My child,

You may have to endure difficult days while traveling on this journey. However, you are not alone. The enemy wants to isolate and torment you. When you feel yourself withdrawing from life, lift up your head, cry out to me, and I will deliver you from the pit of despair.

I Love You ~♥~

John 16:31- 33 (MSG)
Jesus answered them, "Do you finally believe? In fact, you're about to make a run for it—saving your own skins and abandoning me. But I'm not abandoned. The Father is with me. I've told you all this so that trusting me, you will be unshakable and assured, deeply at peace. In this godless world you will continue to experience difficulties. But take heart! I've conquered the world."

Psalm 146:9 (ESV)
The Lord watches over the sojourners; he upholds the widow and the fatherless, but the way of the wicked he brings to ruin.

Psalm 40:1-3 (NLT)
I waited patiently for the Lord to help me, and he turned to me and heard my cry. 2 He lifted me out of the pit of despair, out of the mud and the mire. He set my feet on solid ground and steadied me as I walked along. 3 He has given me a new song to sing, a hymn of praise to our God. Many will see what he has done and be amazed. They will put their trust in the Lord.

My child,

I've heard your question, "how much more am I going to have to take?" I have not placed you here to be anxious over your life. My Kingdom operates in giving and receiving. When you find yourself overwhelmed with life issues, give them to me and receive my strength, power and peace. I'll take it and make it useful for my Kingdom.

I Love You ~♥~

Luke 6:38 (KJV)
Give, and it shall be given unto you; good measure, pressed down, and shaken together, and running over, shall men give into your bosom. For with the same measure that ye mete withal it shall be measured to you again.

Philippians 4:19 (KJV)
"But my God shall supply all your need according to his riches in glory by Christ Jesus."

1 Peter 5:6-11 (MSG)
So be content with who you are, and don't put on airs. God's strong hand is on you; he'll promote you at the right time. Live carefree before God; he is most careful with you. Keep a cool head. Stay alert. The Devil is poised to pounce, and would like nothing better than to catch you napping. Keep your guard up. You're not the only ones plunged into these hard times. It's the same with Christians all over the world. So keep a firm grip on the faith. The suffering won't last forever. It won't be long before this generous God who has great plans for us in Christ—eternal and glorious plans they are!—will have you put together and on your feet for good. He gets the last word; yes, he does.

My Child,

_____
_____
_____
_____
_____
_____
_____
_____
_____
_____
_____
_____
_____
_____
_____
_____
_____
_____
_____
_____
_____
_____
_____
_____
_____
_____
_____

I Love You

~ ~

prayer

WORRIER

or

PRAYER

warrior

My child,

I am always available for you to come boldly to my throne. Do not hesitate to run to me when you stumble or fall. I understand you, and I am not like man, I will never reject you. Do not allow fear to hold you captive any longer. I am the way to your freedom, come back home to me!

I Love You ~♥~

Hebrews 4:16 (NKJV)
Let us therefore come boldly to the throne of grace, that we may obtain mercy and find grace to help in time of need.

Deuteronomy 31:6 (MSG)
"Be strong. Take courage. Don't be intimidated. Don't give them a second thought because God, your God, is striding ahead of you. He's right there with you. He won't let you down; he won't leave you."

1 Peter 2:4 (ESV)
As you come to him, a living stone rejected by men but in the sight of God chosen and precious,

Hebrews 2: 14-15 (MSG)
Since the children are made of flesh and blood, it's logical that the Savior took on flesh and blood in order to rescue them by his death. By embracing death, taking it into himself, he destroyed the Devil's hold on death and freed all who cower through life, scared to death of death.

My child,

Love lifted me up on the cross for you. If you would only believe how much I love you, it would cast out all fear and doubt. I made a way for you to have full access to me. Come, sit with me, commune with me, and share your heart with me. I want to partake in the smallest of details in your life. I am your friend.

I Love You ~♥~

John 12:32 (ESV)
And I, when I am lifted up from the earth, will draw all people to myself."

1 John 4:17-18 (MSG)
God is love. When we take up permanent residence in a life of love, we live in God and God lives in us. This way, love has the run of the house, becomes at home and mature in us, so that we're free of worry on Judgment Day—our standing in the world is identical with Christ's. There is no room in love for fear. Well-formed love banishes fear. Since fear is crippling, a fearful life—fear of death, fear of judgment—is one not yet fully formed in love.

Luke 10:38-42 (NLT)
As Jesus and the disciples continued on their way to Jerusalem, they came to a certain village where a woman named Martha welcomed him into her home. 39 Her sister, Mary, sat at the Lord's feet, listening to what he taught. 40 But Martha was distracted by the big dinner she was preparing. She came to Jesus and said, "Lord, doesn't it seem unfair to you that my sister just sits here while I do all the work? Tell her to come and help me." 41 But the Lord said to her, "My dear Martha, you are worried and upset over all these details! 42 There is only one thing worth being concerned about. Mary has discovered it, and it will not be taken away from her."

My child,

Things are not always as they appear. You must not be too quick to judge. If you ask me, I will help you understand. Anytime you experience confusion, it's time to stop and ask me for clarity. I do not operate in confusion, and neither should you.

I Love You ~♥~

Matthew 7:1-5 (NLT)
"Do not judge others, and you will not be judged. 2 For you will be treated as you treat others. The standard you use in judging is the standard by which you will be judged. 3 "And why worry about a speck in your friend's eye when you have a log in your own? 4 How can you think of saying to your friend, 'Let me help you get rid of that speck in your eye,' when you can't see past the log in your own eye? 5 Hypocrite! First get rid of the log in your own eye; then you will see well enough to deal with the speck in your friend's eye.

1 Corinthians 14:33 (ESV)
For God is not a God of confusion but of peace.

Ephesians 1:15-19 (MSG)
That's why, when I heard of the solid trust you have in the Master Jesus and your outpouring of love to all the followers of Jesus, I couldn't stop thanking God for you—every time I prayed, I'd think of you and give thanks. But I do more than thank. I ask—ask the God of our Master, Jesus Christ, the God of glory—to make you intelligent and discerning in knowing him personally, your eyes focused and clear, so that you can see exactly what it is he is calling you to do, grasp the immensity of this glorious way of life he has for his followers, oh, the utter extravagance of his work in us who trust him—endless energy, boundless strength!

My child,

I know you are growing weary as you walk through difficult days. I am here to walk with you. As you have prayed to be more like me and have opportunities to show others who I am, you will encounter suffering. Don't lose heart, keep pressing on, and don't give up. This world is temporary, my glory is eternal.

I Love You ~♥~

Romans 8:18-28 (MSG)
18-21 That's why I don't think there's any comparison between the present hard times and the coming good times. The created world itself can hardly wait for what's coming next. Everything in creation is being more or less held back. God reins it in until both creation and all the creatures are ready and can be released at the same moment into the glorious times ahead. Meanwhile, the joyful anticipation deepens. 22-25 All around us we observe a pregnant creation. The difficult times of pain throughout the world are simply birth pangs. But it's not only around us; it's within us. The Spirit of God is arousing us within. We're also feeling the birth pangs. These sterile and barren bodies of ours are yearning for full deliverance. That is why waiting does not diminish us, any more than waiting diminishes a pregnant mother. We are enlarged in the waiting. We, of course, don't see what is enlarging us. But the longer we wait, the larger we become, and the more joyful our expectancy. 26-28 meanwhile, the moment we get tired in the waiting, God's Spirit is right alongside helping us along. If we don't know how or what to pray, it doesn't matter. He does our praying in and for us, making prayer out of our wordless sighs, our aching groans. He knows us far better than we know ourselves, knows our pregnant condition, and keeps us present before God. That's why we can be so sure that every detail in our lives of love for God is worked into something good.

My child,

It's time for you to take your rightful place in my Kingdom. You need to acknowledge who I say you are and what authority I say you have. When you operate in my authority, no weapons formed by the adversary can stand against you. I readily give this power to you. You are an overcomer, now live like it!

I Love You ~♥~

2 Corinthians 10:8 (NLT)
I may seem to be boasting too much about the authority given to us by the Lord. But our authority builds you up; it doesn't tear you down. So I will not be ashamed of using my authority.

2 Corinthians 10:4 (ESV)
For the weapons of our warfare are not of the flesh but have divine power to destroy strongholds.

Isaiah 54:17 (NKJV)
"No weapon formed against you shall prosper, And every tongue which rises against you in judgment You shall condemn. This is the heritage of the servants of the Lord, and their righteousness is from Me," Says the Lord.

John 10:25-30 (MSG)
Jesus answered, "I told you, but you don't believe. Everything I have done has been authorized by my Father, actions that speak louder than words. You don't believe because you're not my sheep. My sheep recognize my voice. I know them, and they follow me. I give them real and eternal life. They are protected from the Destroyer for good. No one can steal them from out of my hand. The Father who put them under my care is so much greater than the Destroyer and Thief. No one could ever get them away from him. I and the Father are one heart and mind."

My Child,

I Love You

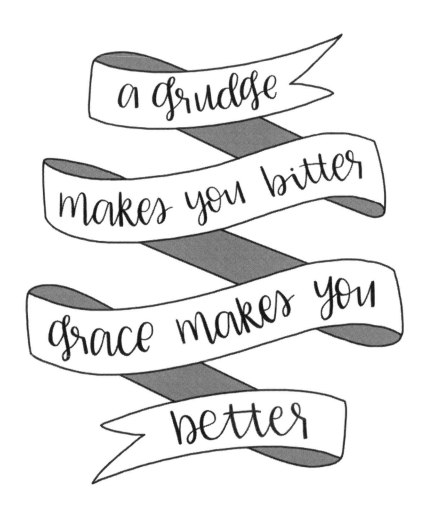

a grudge makes you bitter grace makes you better

My child,

I want your undivided attention. Many times you come to me with half of your heart. I give you my all, and that's what I want from you- your all. Today, stop and spend time with me. Put aside all other distractions and fully focus on me. I am a jealous God, and I will not compete with other gods in your life. You decide today who you will serve. Choose wisely.

I Love You ~♥~

Proverbs 4:20-22 (MSG)
Dear friend, listen well to my words; tune your ears to my voice. Keep my message in plain view at all times. Concentrate! Learn it by heart! Those who discover these words live, really live; body and soul, they're bursting with health.

1 Corinthians 7:32-35 (MSG)
I want you to live as free of complications as possible. When you're unmarried, you're free to concentrate on simply pleasing the Master. Marriage involves you in all the nuts and bolts of domestic life and in wanting to please your spouse, leading to so many more demands on your attention. The time and energy that married people spend on caring for and nurturing each other, the unmarried can spend in becoming whole and holy instruments of God. I'm trying to be helpful and make it as easy as possible for you, not make things harder. All I want is for you to be able to develop a way of life in which you can spend plenty of time together with the Master without a lot of distractions.

My child,

The seasons are changing once again. What has seemed dead to you will now begin to grow again. When you place your hope in me, I will give new life. I have the power to turn this around! Do you believe?

I Love You ~♥~

Ecclesiastes 3:1-8 (KJV)
To everything there is a season, and a time to every purpose under the heaven: 2 A time to be born, and a time to die; a time to plant, and a time to pluck up that which is planted; 3 A time to kill, and a time to heal; a time to break down, and a time to build up; 4 A time to weep, and a time to laugh; a time to mourn, and a time to dance; 5 A time to cast away stones, and a time to gather stones together; a time to embrace, and a time to refrain from embracing; 6 A time to get, and a time to lose; a time to keep, and a time to cast away; 7 A time to rend, and a time to sew; a time to keep silence, and a time to speak; 8 A time to love, and a time to hate; a time of war, and a time of peace.

Ezekiel 36:24-28 (MSG)
"'For here's what I'm going to do: I'm going to take you out of these countries, gather you from all over, and bring you back to your own land. I'll pour pure water over you and scrub you clean. I'll give you a new heart, put a new spirit in you. I'll remove the stone heart from your body and replace it with a heart that's God-willed, not self-willed. I'll put my Spirit in you and make it possible for you to do what I tell you and live by my commands. You'll once again live in the land I gave your ancestors. You'll be my people! I'll be your God!

1 Peter 5:11 (NLV)
God has power over all things forever. Let it be so.

My child,

My grace is sufficient for you. When I see you turning to other things, it demonstrates your lack of faith in me. I will meet all your needs, I will keep my word to you. Look only to me and no other places for your provision, power and peace. I am truly all you need to live victoriously in this life. Putting me first allows my power to work through you!

I Love You ~♥~

2 Corinthians 12:8-10 (NASB)
Concerning this I implored the Lord three times that it might leave me. 9 And He has said to me, "My grace is sufficient for you, for power is perfected in weakness." Most gladly, therefore, I will rather boast about my weaknesses, so that the power of Christ may dwell in me. 10 Therefore I am well content with weaknesses, with insults, with distresses, with persecutions, with difficulties, for Christ's sake; for when I am weak, then I am strong.

Philippians 4:19 (NIV)
And my God will meet all your needs according to the riches of his glory in Christ Jesus.

John 6:37-40 (ESV)
All that the Father gives me will come to me, and whoever comes to me I will never cast out. 38 For I have come down from heaven, not to do my own will but the will of him who sent me. 39 And this is the will of him who sent me, that I should lose nothing of all that he has given me, but raise it up on the last day. 40 For this is the will of my Father, that everyone who looks on the Son and believes in him should have eternal life, and I will raise him up on the last day."

My child,

You can always choose joy. Even in the most difficult times, joy can be found in me! You will experience peace on a deeper level, when you purposely choose joy during difficult times. I am here to bless you.

I Love You ~♥~

James 1:2-4 (HCSB)
Consider it a great joy, my brothers, whenever you experience various trials, 3 knowing that the testing of your faith produces endurance. 4 But endurance must do its complete work, so that you may be mature and complete, lacking nothing.

I
saiah 35:10 (ESV)
And the ransomed of the Lord shall return and come to Zion with singing; everlasting joy shall be upon their heads; they shall obtain gladness and joy, and sorrow and sighing shall flee away.

Nehemiah 8:10 (NIV)
....The Joy of the Lord is my strength.

1 Peter 1:8-9 (NIV)
Though you have not seen him, you love him; and even though you do not see him now, you believe in him and are filled with an inexpressible and glorious joy, 9 for you are receiving the end result of your faith, the salvation of your souls.

Hebrews 12:2 (NIV)
Fixing our eyes on Jesus, the pioneer and perfecter of faith. For the joy set before him he endured the cross, scorning its shame, and sat down at the right hand of the throne of God.

My child,

When you are searching for something, stop and look before you. The answer could possibly be in front of your eyes. Take care to enlist my all- knowing wisdom to direct you. It is not necessary to search far and wide. The answer is here - I AM the answer!

I Love You ~♥~

Matthew 11:25-26 (MSG)
Abruptly Jesus broke into prayer: "Thank you, Father, Lord of heaven and earth. You've concealed your ways from sophisticates and know-it-alls, but spelled them out clearly to ordinary people. Yes, Father, that's the way you like to work."

1 Corinthians 13:12 (ESV)
For now we see in a mirror dimly, but then face to face. Now I know in part; then I shall know fully, even as I have been fully known.

Job 28:13 (NIV)
No mortal comprehends its worth; it cannot be found in the land of the living.

1 Kings 3:6-9 (NIV)
Solomon answered, "You have shown great kindness to your servant, my father David, because he was faithful to you and righteous and upright in heart. You have continued this great kindness to him and have given him a son to sit on his throne this very day. 7 "Now, Lord my God, you have made your servant king in place of my father David. But I am only a little child and do not know how to carry out my duties. 8 Your servant is here among the people you have chosen, a great people, too numerous to count or number. 9 So give your servant a discerning heart to govern your people and to distinguish between right and wrong. For who is able to govern this great people of yours?"

My Child,

I Love You

F.A.I.T.H.

{ for all I trust Him }

My child,

Seldom do you take the time and tarry at my feet. I long for your full undivided attention. Can we just sit together as two friends, enjoying conversations, laughter and sharing life together? You will enjoy our journey through life much better if you choose to slow down and spend more time with me.

I Love You ~♥~

Matthew 26:38-39 (KJV)
Then saith he unto them, My soul is exceeding sorrowful, even unto death: tarry ye here, and watch with me. 39 And he went a little farther, and fell on his face, and prayed, saying, O my Father, if it be possible, let this cup pass from me: nevertheless not as I will, but as thou wilt.

James 2:22-24 (NLT)
You see, his faith and his actions worked together. His actions made his faith complete. 23 And so it happened just as the Scriptures say: "Abraham believed God, and God counted him as righteous because of his faith." He was even called the friend of God. 24 So you see, we are shown to be right with God by what we do, not by faith alone.

Jeremiah 2:25 (MSG)
"Slow down. Take a deep breath. What's the hurry? Why wear yourself out? Just what are you after anyway? But you say, 'I can't help it. I'm addicted to alien gods. I can't quit.'

Colossians 2:6-7 (NLT)
And now, just as you accepted Christ Jesus as your Lord, you must continue to follow him. 7 Let your roots grow down into him, and let your lives be built on him. Then your faith will grow strong in the truth you were taught, and you will overflow with thankfulness.

My child,

Where do you turn in times of trouble? Do you seek me or man? Take time and think about your answer because where you run in uncertain times will show your faith level. Always turn to me first, I will deepen your faith.

I Love You ~♥~

2 Corinthians 4:8-12 (NLT)
We are pressed on every side by troubles, but we are not crushed. We are perplexed, but not driven to despair. 9 We are hunted down, but never abandoned by God. We get knocked down, but we are not destroyed. 10 Through suffering, our bodies continue to share in the death of Jesus so that the life of Jesus may also be seen in our bodies. 11 Yes, we live under constant danger of death because we serve Jesus, so that the life of Jesus will be evident in our dying bodies. 12 So we live in the face of death, but this has resulted in eternal life for you.

Psalm 50:15 (NLT)
Then call on me when you are in trouble, and I will rescue you, and you will give me glory."

Mark 11:22-25 (MSG)
Jesus was matter-of-fact: "Embrace this God-life. Really embrace it, and nothing will be too much for you. This mountain, for instance: Just say, 'Go jump in the lake'—no shuffling or shilly-shallying—and it's as good as done. That's why I urge you to pray for absolutely everything, ranging from small to large. Include everything as you embrace this God-life, and you'll get God's everything. And when you assume the posture of prayer, remember that it's not all asking. If you have anything against someone, forgive—only then will your heavenly Father be inclined to also wipe your slate clean of sins."

My child,

You read my words, but do you believe them to be true in your life? I am the same God, I will never change - I remain constant and true to you. I am no respecter of persons. The instability you're feeling is not from me. I am your strong and mighty tower - run to me and be saved!

I Love you ~♥~

1 Thessalonians 2:13 (NIV)
And we also thank God continually because, when you received the word of God, which you heard from us, you accepted it not as a human word, but as it actually is, the word of God, which is indeed at work in you who believe.

Hebrews 13:8 (ESV)
Jesus Christ is the same yesterday and today and forever.

Acts 10:34-35 (KJV)
Then Peter opened his mouth, and said, Of a truth I perceive that God is no respecter of persons: 35 But in every nation he that feareth him, and worketh righteousness, is accepted with him.

Proverbs 18:10-15 (NIV)
The name of the Lord is a fortified tower; the righteous run to it and are safe. 11 The wealth of the rich is their fortified city; they imagine it a wall too high to scale. 12 Before a downfall the heart is haughty, but humility comes before honor. 13 To answer before listening— that is folly and shame. 14 The human spirit can endure in sickness, but a crushed spirit who can bear? 15 The heart of the discerning acquires knowledge, for the ears of the wise seek it out.

My child,

From the moment I first saw you, I loved you. It hurts my heart when I see you not loving yourself. You have been given unique gifts and talents from me. Don't hold back from using them for my Kingdom. Step into your calling and trust me to provide all that you need to complete the task before you. I Love You ~♥~

1 John 4:18-20 (ESV)
There is no fear in love, but perfect love casts out fear. For fear has to do with punishment, and whoever fears has not been perfected in love. 19 We love because he first loved us. 20 If anyone says, "I love God," and hates his brother, he is a liar; for he who does not love his brother whom he has seen cannot love God whom he has not seen.

James 1:17 (NIV)
Every good and perfect gift is from above, coming down from the Father of the heavenly lights, who does not change like shifting shadows.

2 Timothy 1:8-10 (AMP)
8 So do not be ashamed to testify about our Lord or about me His prisoner, but with me take your share of suffering for the gospel [continue to preach regardless of the circumstances], in accordance with the power of God [for His power is invincible], 9 for He delivered us and saved us and called us with a holy calling [a calling that leads to a consecrated life—a life set apart—a life of purpose], not because of our works [or because of any personal merit—we could do nothing to earn this], but because of His own purpose and grace [His amazing, undeserved favor] which was granted to us in Christ Jesus before the world began [eternal ages ago], 10 but now [that extraordinary purpose and grace] has been fully disclosed and realized by us through the appearing of our Savior Christ Jesus who [through His incarnation and earthly ministry] abolished death [making it null and void] and brought life and immortality to light through the gospel,

My child,

It is my desire for you to abide in my perfect peace. When you exercise your faith, fear is not a factor. I have never, nor would I ever, abandon you. I have plans for you; trust me, believe me and obey me.

I Love you ~♥~

Isaiah 26:3 (AMP)
"You will keep in perfect and constant peace the one whose mind is steadfast [that is, committed and focused on You—in both inclination and character], Because he trusts and takes refuge in You [with hope and confident expectation]."

2 Peter 1:5-9 (MSG)
So don't lose a minute in building on what you've been given, complementing your basic faith with good character, spiritual understanding, alert discipline, passionate patience, reverent wonder, warm friendliness, and generous love, each dimension fitting into and developing the others. With these qualities active and growing in your lives, no grass will grow under your feet, no day will pass without its reward as you mature in your experience of our Master Jesus. Without these qualities you can't see what's right before you, oblivious that your old sinful life has been wiped off the books.

Romans 2:6-8 (ESV)
He will render to each one according to his works: 7 to those who by patience in well-doing seek for glory and honor and immortality, he will give eternal life; 8 but for those who are self-seeking and do not obey the truth, but obey unrighteousness, there will be wrath and fury.

My Child,

I Love You

CAST YOUR CARES DON'T CARRY THEM

My child,

You need to place your hand in mine and hold to me. When you experience unsettling times, my unchanging hand will steady you. I will never let go of you, please never let go of me. I am your only hope. This world and all that is in it at some point will disappoint you.

I Love You ~♥~

Psalm 25:1-3 (ERV)
Lord, I put my life in your hands. 2 I trust in you, my God, and I will not be disappointed. My enemies will not laugh at me. 3 No one who trusts in you will be disappointed. But disappointment will come to those who try to deceive others. They will get nothing.

Hebrews 13:5-6 (MSG)
Don't be obsessed with getting more material things. Be relaxed with what you have. Since God assured us, "I'll never let you down, never walk off and leave you," we can boldly quote, God is there, ready to help; I'm fearless no matter what. Who or what can get to me?

Romans 5:2-7 (NIV)
Through whom we have gained access by faith into this grace in which we now stand. And we boast in the hope of the glory of God. 3 Not only so, but we also glory in our sufferings, because we know that suffering produces perseverance; 4 perseverance, character; and character, hope. 5 And hope does not put us to shame, because God's love has been poured out into our hearts through the Holy Spirit, who has been given to us. 6 You see, at just the right time, when we were still powerless, Christ died for the ungodly. 7 Very rarely will anyone die for a righteous person, though for a good person someone might possibly dare to die.

My child,

You have invited me in to be your personal saviour, yet you try and save yourself. When life becomes difficult, you try to work out your own plan. I call you to be anxious for nothing and that's what I truly mean. Do not worry about anything, you do not need control when I am in control. Trust me, alone!

I Love You ~♥~

John 3:16 (KJV)
For God so loved the world, that he gave his only begotten Son, that whosoever believeth in him should not perish, but have everlasting life.

Mark 10:21 (NASB)
Looking at him, Jesus felt a love for him and said to him, "One thing you lack: go and sell all you possess and give to the poor, and you will have treasure in heaven; and come, follow Me."

Isaiah 45:6-7 (ESV)
that people may know, from the rising of the sun and from the west, that there is none besides me; I am the Lord, and there is no other. 7 I form light and create darkness, I make well-being and create calamity, I am the Lord, who does all these things.

Philippians 4:6-7 (MSG)
Don't fret or worry. Instead of worrying, pray. Let petitions and praises shape your worries into prayers, letting God know your concerns. Before you know it, a sense of God's wholeness, everything coming together for good, will come and settle you down. It's wonderful what happens when Christ displaces worry at the center of your life.

My child,

What are you thankful for? I know this world you live in is full of hurt, confusion and oppression. I want your confession to be one of thankfulness. You can be grateful in all things. You can give me thanks for all things and all things to come. Today, my child, I want to hear you say "Thank you, Daddy!"

I Love You ~♥~

Psalm 34(KJV)
I will bless the Lord at all times: his praise shall continually be in my mouth. 2 My soul shall make her boast in the Lord: the humble shall hear thereof, and be glad. 3 O magnify the Lord with me, and let us exalt his name together. 4 I sought the Lord, and he heard me, and delivered me from all my fears. 5 They looked unto him, and were lightened: and their faces were not ashamed. 6 This poor man cried, and the Lord heard him, and saved him out of all his troubles. 7 The angel of the Lord encampeth round about them that fear him, and delivereth them. 8 O taste and see that the Lord is good: blessed is the man that trusteth in him. 9 O fear the Lord, ye his saints: for there is no want to them that fear him. 10 The young lions do lack, and suffer hunger: but they that seek the Lord shall not want any good thing. 11 Come, ye children, hearken unto me: I will teach you the fear of the Lord. 12 What man is he that desireth life, and loveth many days, that he may see good? 13 Keep thy tongue from evil, and thy lips from speaking guile. 14 Depart from evil, and do good; seek peace, and pursue it. 15 The eyes of the Lord are upon the righteous, and his ears are open unto their cry. 16 The face of the Lord is against them that do evil, to cut off the remembrance of them from the earth. 17 The righteous cry, and the Lord heareth, and delivereth them out of all their troubles. 18 The Lord is nigh unto them that are of a broken heart; and saveth such as be of a contrite spirit. 19 Many are the afflictions of the righteous: but the Lord delivereth him out of them all. 20 He keepeth all his bones: not one of them is broken. 21 Evil shall slay the wicked: and they that hate the righteous shall be desolate. 22 The Lord redeemeth the soul of his servants: and none of them that trust in him shall be desolate.

My child,

It is time for you to come and sit in the mercy seat. This is the place where you not only receive mercy, but you give mercy to others. When you're sitting in judgement of others, you are harshly judging yourself. I am calling you to abide in my mercy and follow my plan of redemption over your life.

I Love You ~♥~

Romans 3:23-26 (NLT)
For everyone has sinned; we all fall short of God's glorious standard. 24 Yet God, in his grace, freely makes us right in his sight. He did this through Christ Jesus when he freed us from the penalty for our sins. 25 For God presented Jesus as the sacrifice for sin. People are made right with God when they believe that Jesus sacrificed his life, shedding his blood. This sacrifice shows that God was being fair when he held back and did not punish those who sinned in times past, 26 for he was looking ahead and including them in what he would do in this present time. God did this to demonstrate his righteousness, for he himself is fair and just, and he makes sinners right in his sight when they believe in Jesus.

Luke 6:37-38 (NLT)
"Do not judge others, and you will not be judged. Do not condemn others, or it will all come back against you. Forgive others, and you will be forgiven. 38 Give, and you will receive. Your gift will return to you in full—pressed down, shaken together to make room for more, running over, and poured into your lap. The amount you give will determine the amount you get back."

My child,

It is my desire for you to seek my face, to come boldly before the throne and receive from me. I am a mighty God and I will take care of you. When you walk in the fullness of your faith, all fear, anxiety and doubt is removed. Seek my face, find your grace.

I Love You ~♥~

Hebrews 4:16 (NKJV)
Let us therefore come boldly to the throne of grace, that we may obtain mercy and find grace to help in time of need.

Psalm 27:7-12 (MSG)
Listen, God, I'm calling at the top of my lungs: "Be good to me! Answer me!" When my heart whispered, "Seek God," my whole being replied, "I'm seeking him!" Don't hide from me now! 9-10 You've always been right there for me; don't turn your back on me now. Don't throw me out, don't abandon me; you've always kept the door open. My father and mother walked out and left me, but God took me in. 11-12 Point me down your highway, God; direct me along a well-lighted street; show my enemies whose side you're on. Don't throw me to the dogs, those liars who are out to get me, filling the air with their threats.

2 Corinthians 12:9 (ESV)
But he said to me, "My grace is sufficient for you, for my power is made perfect in weakness." Therefore I will boast all the more gladly of my weaknesses, so that the power of Christ may rest upon me.

My Child,

I Love You

perceive THE promise

My child,

If you allow me, I will direct your steps. When you follow my plans, everything works together for the good. When you are being led astray by the trappings of this world, no peace can be found. If you are unclear about directions, ask me. I will never send you down the wrong path.

I Love You ~♥~

1 Samuel 2:9 (NIV)
He will guard the feet of his faithful servants, but the wicked will be silenced in the place of darkness. "It is not by strength that one prevails;"

Psalm 18:19 (NIV)
He brought me out into a spacious place; he rescued me because he delighted in me.

Psalm 25:12 (NIV)
Who, then, are those who fear the LORD? He will instruct them in the ways they should choose.

Psalm 86:11 (HCSB)
Teach me Your way, Lord, and I will live by Your truth. Give me an undivided mind to fear Your name.

My child,

I have made this day for you. Use time throughout your day to praise me. There will always be distractions and obstacles to maneuver through, still praise me anyway! I love to hear your worship, I love seeing your heart trusting me. You are my delight and special treasure!

I Love You ~♥~

Psalm 118:24 (ESV)
This is the day that the Lord has made; let us rejoice and be glad in it.

1 Corinthians 7:35 (HCSB)
Now I am saying this for your own benefit, not to put a restraint on you, but because of what is proper and so that you may be devoted to the Lord without distraction.

1 Chronicles 16:23-31 (NIV)
Sing to the LORD, all the earth; proclaim his salvation day after day. 24 Declare his glory among the nations, his marvelous deeds among all peoples. 25 For great is the LORD and most worthy of praise; he is to be feared above all gods. 26 For all the gods of the nations are idols, but the LORD made the heavens. 27 Splendor and majesty are before him; strength and joy are in his dwelling place. 28 Ascribe to the LORD, all you families of nations, ascribe to the LORD glory and strength. 29 Ascribe to the LORD the glory due his name; bring an offering and come before him. Worship the LORD in the splendor of his holiness. 30 Tremble before him, all the earth! The world is firmly established; it cannot be moved. 31 Let the heavens rejoice, let the earth be glad; let them say among the nations, "The LORD reigns!"

My child,

Your proclamation must be "I shall not be moved!" You must be like a tree planted by the water. Regardless of the environment that surrounds you, you stand firm. Standing firm with the assurance that I am the Lord your God, your protector!

I Love You ~♥~

Jeremiah 17:8 (NLT)
They are like trees planted along a riverbank, with roots that reach deep into the water. Such trees are not bothered by the heat or worried by long months of drought. Their leaves stay green, and they never stop producing fruit.

Psalm 3 (KJV)
Lord, how are they increased that trouble me! many are they that rise up against me.2 Many there be which say of my soul, There is no help for him in God. Selah. 3 But thou, O Lord, art a shield for me; my glory, and the lifter up of mine head. 4 I cried unto the Lord with my voice, and he heard me out of his holy hill. Selah. 5 I laid me down and slept; I awaked; for the Lord sustained me. 6 I will not be afraid of ten thousands of people, that have set themselves against me round about. 7 Arise, O Lord; save me, O my God: for thou hast smitten all mine enemies upon the cheek bone; thou hast broken the teeth of the ungodly. 8 Salvation belongeth unto the Lord: thy blessing is upon thy people. Selah.

2 Samuel 22:31 (KJV)
As for God, his way is perfect; the word of the Lord is tried: he is a buckler to all them that trust in him.

My child,

Putting on love is a choice. This world wants you to wear bitterness, anger, jealousy, resentfulness, judgement, envy, hate; this is not my will for your life. Once again, I tell you putting on love is your choice. Love never fails - Love is greater - Choose Love! I Love You ~♥~

Colossians 3:14-17 (ESV)
And above all these put on love, which binds everything together in perfect harmony. 15 And let the peace of Christ rule in your hearts, to which indeed you were called in one body. And be thankful. 16 Let the word of Christ dwell in you richly, teaching and admonishing one another in all wisdom, singing psalms and hymns and spiritual songs, with thankfulness in your hearts to God. 17 And whatever you do, in word or deed, do everything in the name of the Lord Jesus, giving thanks to God the Father through him.

1 Corinthians 13:1-13 (ESV)
 If I speak in the tongues of men and of angels, but have not love, I am a noisy gong or a clanging cymbal. 2 And if I have prophetic powers, and understand all mysteries and all knowledge, and if I have all faith, so as to remove mountains, but have not love, I am nothing. 3 If I give away all I have, and if I deliver up my body to be burned, but have not love, I gain nothing. 4 Love is patient and kind; love does not envy or boast; it is not arrogant 5 or rude. It does not insist on its own way; it is not irritable or resentful; 6 it does not rejoice at wrongdoing, but rejoices with the truth. 7 Love bears all things, believes all things, hopes all things, endures all things. 8 Love never ends. As for prophecies, they will pass away; as for tongues, they will cease; as for knowledge, it will pass away. 9 For we know in part and we prophesy in part, 10 but when the perfect comes, the partial will pass away. 11 When I was a child, I spoke like a child, I thought like a child, I reasoned like a child. When I became a man, I gave up childish ways. 12 For now we see in a mirror dimly, but then face to face. Now I know in part; then I shall know fully, even as I have been fully known. 13 So now faith, hope, and love abide, these three; but the greatest of these is love.

My child,

Sometimes it is necessary for me to be quiet. Even in times of my silence, you still have my word. When your heart is being tested, you can remain confident. Don't become anxious and give up. Stay close to me and know I am working on your behalf. Keep walking in my word, and I will lead you home.

I Love You ~♥~

Zephaniah 3:17 (NASB)
"The LORD your God is in your midst, A victorious warrior He will exult over you with joy, He will be quiet in His love, He will rejoice over you with shouts of joy."

Deuteronomy 8:1-5 (MSG)
Keep and live out the entire commandment that I'm commanding you today so that you'll live and prosper and enter and own the land that God promised to your ancestors. Remember every road that God led you on for those forty years in the wilderness, pushing you to your limits, testing you so that he would know what you were made of, whether you would keep his commandments or not. He put you through hard times. He made you go hungry. Then he fed you with manna, something neither you nor your parents knew anything about, so you would learn that men and women don't live by bread only; we live by every word that comes from God's mouth. Your clothes didn't wear out and your feet didn't blister those forty years. You learned deep in your heart that God disciplines you in the same ways a father disciplines his child.

Matthew 6:19-21 (AMP)
"Do not store up for yourselves [material] treasures on earth, where moth and rust destroy, and where thieves break in and steal. But store up for yourselves treasures in heaven, where neither moth nor rust destroys, and where thieves do not break in and steal; for where your treasure is, there your heart [your wishes; that on which your life centers] will be also.

My Child,

I Love You

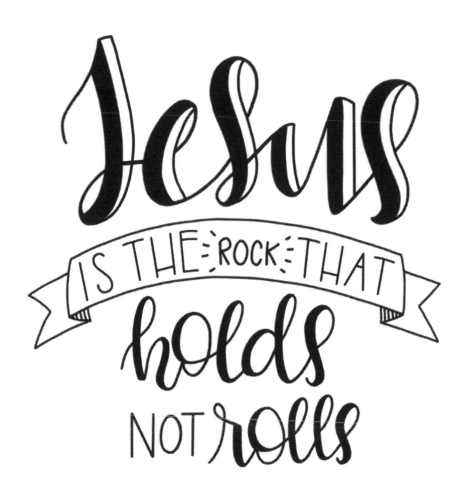

Jesus is the rock that holds not rolls

My child,

Stay the course. You have come too far to stop or turn back. Turning back only takes you to places that you needed to leave behind you. When you live, move, and have your life in me, together we move forward. Keep pressing on to what is in front of you. No turning back. I Love You ~♥~

Psalm 119:1-8 (MSG)
You're blessed when you stay on course, walking steadily on the road revealed by God. You're blessed when you follow his directions, doing your best to find him. That's right - you don't go off on your own; you walk straight along the road he set. You, God, prescribed the right way to live; now you expect us to live it. Oh, that my steps might be steady, keeping to the course you set; Then I'd never have any regrets in comparing my life with your counsel. I thank you for speaking straight from your heart; I learn the pattern of your righteous ways. I'm going to do what you tell me to do; don't ever walk off and leave me.

Philippians 3:12-14 (MSG)
I'm not saying that I have this all together, that I have it made. But I am well on my way, reaching out for Christ, who has so wondrously reached out for me. Friends, don't get me wrong: By no means do I count myself an expert in all of this, but I've got my eye on the goal, where God is beckoning us onward—to Jesus. I'm off and running, and I'm not turning back.

Acts 17:28 (NLT)
For in him we live and move and exist. As some of your own poets have said, 'We are his offspring.'

Ephesians 4:21-23 (NLT)
Since you have heard about Jesus and have learned the truth that comes from him, throw off your old sinful nature and your former way of life, which is corrupted by lust and deception. Instead, let the Spirit renew your thoughts and attitudes.

My child,

I've called you out of the darkness into my light. There will be no more "little white lies." Either you tell the truth or you're in deception. I call you to abide in truth, my truth. My truth will always set you free and you will be free, indeed!

I Love You ~♥~

1 Peter 2:9 (NIV)
But you are a chosen people, a royal priesthood, a holy nation, God's special possession, that you may declare the praises of him who called you out of darkness into his wonderful light.

Ephesians 5:5-6 (ESV)
For you may be sure of this, that everyone who is sexually immoral or impure, or who is covetous (that is, an idolater), has no inheritance in the kingdom of Christ and God. 6 Let no one deceive you with empty words, for because of these things the wrath of God comes upon the sons of disobedience.

Colossians 3:15-17 (MSG)
Let the peace of Christ keep you in tune with each other, in step with each other. None of this going off and doing your own thing. And cultivate thankfulness. Let the Word of Christ—the Message—have the run of the house. Give it plenty of room in your lives. Instruct and direct one another using good common sense. And sing, sing your hearts out to God! Let every detail in your lives—words, actions, whatever—be done in the name of the Master, Jesus, thanking God the Father every step of the way.

John 8:31-32 (HCSB)
So Jesus said to the Jews who had believed Him, "If you continue in My word, you really are My disciples. 32 You will know the truth, and the truth will set you free."

My child,

I've called you to be free. In my freedom you will have to relinquish and release false comforts. False comforts can be anything you turn to for relief instead of seeking me. I made a way for you to overcome! Follow me and find true freedom!

I Love You ~♥~

Ephesians 2:8-10 (ESV)
For by grace you have been saved through faith. And this is not your own doing; it is the gift of God, 9 not a result of works, so that no one may boast. 10 For we are his workmanship, created in Christ Jesus for good works, which God prepared beforehand, that we should walk in them.

Job 21:34 (MSG)
"So how do you expect me to get any comfort from your nonsense? Your
so-called comfort is a tissue of lies."

John 16:33 (KJV)
These things I have spoken unto you, that in me ye might have peace. In the world ye shall have tribulation: but be of good cheer; I have overcome the world.

Revelation 12:11 (AMP)
And they overcame and conquered him because of the blood of the Lamb and because of the word of their testimony, for they did not love their life and renounce their faith even when faced with death.

My child,

You are not a mistake! I have never made a mistake. Stop agreeing with the lies that have been spoken over you, and know that I planned your life. It is time for you to live the abundant life that I have for you. I love to hear you speak blessings over your life. I enjoy seeing you smile and choosing to be joyful, even when you could be sad. Trusting and believing me is exercising your faith, and your faith is pleasing to me.

I Love You ~♥~

Ephesians 1:3-6 (MSG)
How blessed is God! And what a blessing he is! He's the Father of our Master, Jesus Christ, and takes us to the high places of blessing in him. Long before he laid down earth's foundations, he had us in mind, had settled on us as the focus of his love, to be made whole and holy by his love. Long, long ago he decided to adopt us into his family through Jesus Christ. (What pleasure he took in planning this!) He wanted us to enter into the celebration of his lavish gift-giving by the hand of his beloved Son.

Ephesians 4:22-24 (NLT)
...throw off your old sinful nature and your former way of life, which is corrupted by lust and deception. 23 Instead, let the Spirit renew your thoughts and attitudes. 24 Put on your new nature, created to be like God—truly righteous and holy.

1 Thessalonians 5:16-18 (NLT)
Always be joyful. 17 Never stop praying. 18 Be thankful in all circumstances, for this is God's will for you who belong to Christ Jesus.

Hebrews 11:6 (HCSB)
Now without faith it is impossible to please God, for the one who draws near to Him must believe that He exists and rewards those who seek Him.

My child,

It is time for you to give me your complete heart. No longer can your heart be divided. Divided by or among people, places, positions, power, prestige or pleasures. When you bring me all of your heart, then you will know me in all of my fullness. Let it all go and let me be enough.

I Love You~♥~

Deuteronomy 6:5 (NLT)
And you must love the LORD your God with all your heart, all your soul, and all your strength.

Matthew 22:37 (ESV)
And he said to him, "You shall love the Lord your God with all your heart and with all your soul and with all your mind.

Mark 12:30-31 (MSG)
Jesus said, "The first in importance is, 'Listen, Israel: The Lord your God is one; so love the Lord God with all your passion and prayer and intelligence and energy.' And here is the second: 'Love others as well as you love yourself.' There is no other commandment that ranks with these."

Hosea 10:2 (KJV)
Their heart is divided; now shall they be found faulty: he shall break down their altars, he shall spoil their images.

James 1:5-8 (MSG)
If you don't know what you're doing, pray to the Father. He loves to help. You'll get his help, and won't be condescended to when you ask for it. Ask boldly, believingly, without a second thought. People who "worry their prayers" are like wind-whipped waves. Don't think you're going to get anything from the Master that way, adrift at sea, keeping all your options open.

My Child,

I Love You

you'll want for NOTHING WHEN God IS YOUR everything

My child,

You cannot continue at the pace you are living. It is time for you to slow down and reevaluate your priorities. Our time together is the first thing to suffer because of your lack of time. Don't you realize that I hold your time in my hands? Time is a gift that I give to you. Please start spending it wisely and give back to me a little of what I bless you with. I want your undivided attention.

I Love You ~♥~

Psalm 90:12 (AMP)
So teach us to number our days, That we may cultivate and bring to You a heart of wisdom.

Ephesians 5:16 (ESV)
...making the best use of the time, because the days are evil.

Psalm 31:15 (HCSB)
The course of my life is in Your power; deliver me from the power of my enemies and from my persecutors.

Joshua 10:12-15 (NASB)
Then Joshua spoke to the Lord in the day when the Lord delivered up the Amorites before the sons of Israel, and he said in the sight of Israel, "O sun, stand still at Gibeon, And O moon in the valley of Aijalon." So the sun stood still, and the moon stopped, Until the nation avenged themselves of their enemies. Is it not written in the book of Jashar? And the sun stopped in the middle of the sky and did not hasten to go down for about a whole day. There was no day like that before it or after it, when the Lord listened to the voice of a man; for the Lord fought for Israel. Then Joshua and all Israel with him returned to the camp to Gilgal.

1 Corinthians 7:35 (TLB)
I am saying this to help you, not to try to keep you from marrying. I want you to do whatever will help you serve the Lord best, with as few other things as possible to distract your attention from him.

My child,

I am always with you. My love for you has no boundaries. You cannot measure my love by your earthly encounters. My love is steadfast and pure. My love is everlasting and will endure. I want you to settle down and rest in my love - you are safe here!

I Love You ~♥~

Romans 8:38-39 (ESV)
For I am sure that neither death nor life, nor angels nor rulers, nor things present nor things to come, nor powers, 39 nor height nor depth, nor anything else in all creation, will be able to separate us from the love of God in Christ Jesus our Lord.

Ephesians 3:14-21 (ESV)
For this reason I bow my knees before the Father, 15 from whom every family in heaven and on earth is named, 16 that according to the riches of his glory he may grant you to be strengthened with power through his Spirit in your inner being, 17 so that Christ may dwell in your hearts through faith—that you, being rooted and grounded in love, 18 may have strength to comprehend with all the saints what is the breadth and length and height and depth, 19 and to know the love of Christ that surpasses knowledge, that you may be filled with all the fullness of God. 20 Now to him who is able to do far more abundantly than all that we ask or think, according to the power at work within us, 21 to him be glory in the church and in Christ Jesus throughout all generations, forever and ever. Amen.

Hebrews 13:5-6 (MSG)
Don't be obsessed with getting more material things. Be relaxed with what you have. Since God assured us, "I'll never let you down, never walk off and leave you," we can boldly quote, God is there, ready to help; I'm fearless no matter what. Who or what can get to me?

My child,

The time has come for my true worshippers to arise. Your worship breaks the bondage that holds you as a slave. I am calling you to freedom. Today, regardless of how you feel, worship me in Spirit and truth - and you will be free!

I Love You ~♥~

John 4:23-24 (NLT)
But the time is coming—indeed it's here now—when true worshipers will worship the Father in spirit and in truth. The Father is looking for those who will worship him that way. 24 For God is Spirit, so those who worship him must worship in spirit and in truth."

2 Chronicles 20:5-9 (MSG)
Then Jehoshaphat took a position before the assembled people of Judah and Jerusalem at The Temple of God in front of the new courtyard and said, "O God, God of our ancestors, are you not God in heaven above and ruler of all kingdoms below? You hold all power and might in your fist—no one stands a chance against you! And didn't you make the natives of this land leave as you brought your people Israel in, turning it over permanently to your people Israel, the descendants of Abraham your friend? They have lived here and built a holy house of worship to honor you, saying, 'When the worst happens—whether war or flood or disease or famine—and we take our place before this Temple (we know you are personally present in this place!) and pray out our pain and trouble, we know that you will listen and give victory.'

Galatians 5:1 (ESV)
For freedom Christ has set us free; stand firm therefore, and do not submit again to a yoke of slavery.

My child,

I've heard your cries in the night. Your tears communicate to me, it is a language I understand. As you cry, you experience cleansing and release in areas that need healing. Just like the dry land is nurtured by rain, your tears replenish your soul.

I Love You ~♥~

Psalm 30:5 (KJV)
For his anger endureth but a moment; in his favour is life: weeping may endure for a night, but joy cometh in the morning.

Mark 9:24 (AMP)
Immediately the father of the boy cried out [with a desperate, piercing cry], saying, "I do believe; help [me overcome] my unbelief."

Psalm 126:5 (KJV)
They that sow in tears shall reap in joy.

Jeremiah 31:25 (ESV)
"For I will satisfy the weary soul, and every languishing soul I will replenish."

My child,

Today will you take a few minutes and reflect on where you have been? Do you recognize that through the valley low and the mountain high, I am with you? Your eyes will be opened and you will see with clear vision the purpose of the past and the plans for the future. Trust me alone and believe I AM GOD!

I Love You ~♥~

Isaiah 42:16 (NIV)
I will lead the blind by ways they have not known, along unfamiliar paths I will guide them; I will turn the darkness into light before them and make the rough places smooth. These are the things I will do; I will not forsake them.

Hebrews 13:5 (ESV)
Keep your life free from love of money, and be content with what you have, for he has said, "I will never leave you nor forsake you."

Jeremiah 29:10-11 (MSG)
This is God's Word on the subject: "As soon as Babylon's seventy years are up and not a day before, I'll show up and take care of you as I promised and bring you back home. I know what I'm doing. I have it all planned out—plans to take care of you, not abandon you, plans to give you the future you hope for.

Psalm 56:11 (KJV)
In God have I put my trust: I will not be afraid what man can do unto me.

My Child,

_____
_____
_____
_____
_____
_____
_____
_____
_____
_____
_____
_____
_____
_____
_____
_____
_____
_____
_____
_____
_____
_____
_____
_____
_____
_____
_____
_____

I Love You

My child,
You are beautiful! I have created you from the inside out, giving you special gifts and talents to use for my Kingdom. You are unique and have special ways about you. I know the inward struggles you have with embracing your true identity. Let your beauty shine through your heart to show the world a reflection of me.

I Love You ~♥~

Song of Solomon 4:7 (ESV)
You are altogether beautiful, my love; there is no flaw in you.

Ephesians 2:10 (AMP)
For we are His workmanship [His own master work, a work of art], created in Christ Jesus [reborn from above—spiritually transformed, renewed, ready to be used] for good works, which God prepared [for us] beforehand [taking paths which He set], so that we would walk in them [living the good life which He prearranged and made ready for us].

1 Peter 4:10-11 (ESV)
As each has received a gift, use it to serve one another, as good stewards of God's varied grace: 11 whoever speaks, as one who speaks oracles of God; whoever serves, as one who serves by the strength that God supplies—in order that in everything God may be glorified through Jesus Christ. To him belong glory and dominion forever and ever. Amen.

1 Peter 4:14-16 (MSG)
If you're abused because of Christ, count yourself fortunate. It's the Spirit of God and his glory in you that brought you to the notice of others. If they're on you because you broke the law or disturbed the peace, that's a different matter. But if it's because you're a Christian, don't give it a second thought. Be proud of the distinguished status reflected in that name!

My child,

I have forgiven you. It's time for you to receive my forgiveness and release all your transgressions. Trust me to make right all that is wrong. You stay close to me and walk in my will for your life. Believe me when I say, "I got this."

I Love You ~♥~

1 John 1:9 (AMP)
If we [freely] admit that we have sinned and confess our sins, He is faithful and just [true to His own nature and promises], and will forgive our sins and cleanse us continually from all unrighteousness [our wrongdoing, everything not in conformity with His will and purpose].

John 3:16 (ESV)
"For God so loved the world, that he gave his only Son, that whoever believes in him should not perish but have eternal life."

Ephesians 4:31-32 (MSG)
Make a clean break with all cutting, backbiting, profane talk. Be gentle with one another, sensitive. Forgive one another as quickly and thoroughly as God in Christ forgave you.

Isaiah 55:8-11 (NLT)
"My thoughts are nothing like your thoughts," says the Lord. "And my ways are far beyond anything you could imagine. 9 For just as the heavens are higher than the earth, so my ways are higher than your ways and my thoughts higher than your thoughts. 10 The rain and snow come down from the heavens and stay on the ground to water the earth. They cause the grain to grow, producing seed for the farmer and bread for the hungry. 11 It is the same with my word. I send it out, and it always produces fruit. It will accomplish all I want it to, and it will prosper everywhere I send it."

My child,

Take it one day at a time. When trials come, resist the urge to figure it out and have all the answers. Live in the moment, follow faith and trust me to lead you. You will have times in your life that will not make sense. Don't get distracted with trying to find answers - seek me and be satisfied with not knowing it all.

I Love You ~♥~

Matthew 6:34 (MSG)
"Give your entire attention to what God is doing right now, and don't get worked up about what may or may not happen tomorrow. God will help you deal with whatever hard things come up when the time comes."

Hebrews 6:18-19 (NLT)
So God has given both his promise and his oath. These two things are unchangeable because it is impossible for God to lie. Therefore, we who have fled to him for refuge can have great confidence as we hold to the hope that lies before us. 19 This hope is a strong and trustworthy anchor for our souls. It leads us through the curtain into God's inner sanctuary.

James 1:25 (MSG)
But whoever catches a glimpse of the revealed counsel of God—the free life!—even out of the corner of his eye, and sticks with it, is no distracted scatterbrain but a man or woman of action. That person will find delight and affirmation in the action.

2 Corinthians 5:7 (ESV)
...for we walk by faith, not by sight.

My child,

It's time for you to walk in my favor. Every day I send special favor to your life. You need to slow down and recognize my presence is with you. I always want the best for you. Take a few moments today and seek me. I promise you will find me - I am near!

I Love You ~♥~

Proverbs 8:35 (NKJV)
For whoever finds me finds life, And obtains favor from the Lord;

Zephaniah 3:17 (HCSB)
Yahweh your God is among you, a warrior who saves. He will rejoice over you with gladness. He will bring you quietness with His love.
He will delight in you with shouts of joy.

Psalm 14:2 (NIV)
The LORD looks down from heaven on all mankind to see if there are any who understand, any who seek God.

Psalm 95:6-11 (MSG)
So come, let us worship: bow before him, on your knees before God, who made us! Oh yes, he's our God, and we're the people he pastures, the flock he feeds. Drop everything and listen, listen as he speaks: "Don't turn a deaf ear as in the Bitter Uprising, As on the day of the Wilderness Test, when your ancestors turned and put me to the test. For forty years they watched me at work among them, as over and over they tried my patience. And I was provoked—oh, was I provoked! 'Can't they keep their minds on God for five minutes? Do they simply refuse to walk down my road?' Exasperated, I exploded,' They'll never get where they're headed, never be able to sit down and rest.'"

My child,

If the birds can trust me to provide for their needs, why can't you? You can let go of this and turn it over to me. And when you do, you will not only find peace but answers. Allow me to show you how much I care for you - you are safe with me.

I Love You ~♥~

Matthew 6:25-30 (ESV)
"Therefore I tell you, do not be anxious about your life, what you will eat or what you will drink, nor about your body, what you will put on. Is not life more than food, and the body more than clothing? 26 Look at the birds of the air: they neither sow nor reap nor gather into barns, and yet your heavenly Father feeds them. Are you not of more value than they? 27 And which of you by being anxious can add a single hour to his span of life? 28 And why are you anxious about clothing? Consider the lilies of the field, how they grow: they neither toil nor spin, 29 yet I tell you, even Solomon in all his glory was not arrayed like one of these. 30 But if God so clothes the grass of the field, which today is alive and tomorrow is thrown into the oven, will he not much more clothe you, O you of little faith?"

Psalm 112:7 (KJV)
He shall not be afraid of evil tidings: his heart is fixed, trusting in the Lord.

Genesis 35:3 (ESV)
Then let us arise and go up to Bethel, so that I may make there an altar to the God who answers me in the day of my distress and has been with me wherever I have gone.

Deuteronomy 11:12 (AMP)
...a land for which the Lord your God cares; the eyes of the Lord your God are always on it, from the beginning of the year to the end of the year.

My Child,

_____
_____
_____
_____
_____
_____
_____
_____
_____
_____
_____
_____
_____
_____
_____
_____
_____
_____
_____
_____
_____
_____
_____
_____
_____
_____
_____
_____

I Love You

~♥~

prayer your FIRST response or LAST resort

My child,

There's coming a time when my church will have to stand united as one with me. There is too much division among you as brother and sisters. Find common ground and build upon the foundation of faith. Put aside your differences, and focus on Kingdom work. Don't worry about who is right or wrong. If you are abiding in what I've called of you, then you are right where I want you!

I Love You ~♥~

Colossians 3:14-16 (ESV)
And above all these put on love, which binds everything together in perfect harmony. 15 And let the peace of Christ rule in your hearts, to which indeed you were called in one body. And be thankful. 16 Let the word of Christ dwell in you richly, teaching and admonishing one another in all wisdom, singing psalms and hymns and spiritual songs, with thankfulness in your hearts to God.

1 Corinthians 1:10-16 (MSG)
I have a serious concern to bring up with you, my friends, using the authority of Jesus, our Master. I'll put it as urgently as I can: You must get along with each other. You must learn to be considerate of one another, cultivating a life in common. 11-12 I bring this up because some from Chloe's family brought a most disturbing report to my attention—that you're fighting among yourselves! I'll tell you exactly what I was told: You're all picking sides, going around saying, "I'm on Paul's side," or "I'm for Apollos," or "Peter is my man," or "I'm in the Messiah group."
13-16 I ask you, "Has the Messiah been chopped up in little pieces so we can each have a relic all our own? Was Paul crucified for you? Was a single one of you baptized in Paul's name?" I was not involved with any of your baptisms—except for Crispus and Gaius—and on getting this report, I'm sure glad I wasn't. At least no one can go around saying he was baptized in my name. (Come to think of it, I also baptized Stephanas's family, but as far as I can recall, that's it.)

Matthew 16:18 (KJV)
And I say also unto thee, That thou art Peter, and upon this rock I will build my church; and the gates of hell shall not prevail against it.

My child,

My love for you is like a security blanket. You can wrap up in my love. You can get lost in my love. My love for you brings warmth to your life in the coldest of times. My love for you is a soft place to fall in this rocky and hard world. My love for you never fails. It's enduring, everlasting, full of hope, radiant with joy and always available to you.

I Love You ~♥~

Mark 10:13-16 (MSG)
The people brought children to Jesus, hoping he might touch them. The disciples shooed them off. But Jesus was irate and let them know it: "Don't push these children away. Don't ever get between them and me. These children are at the very center of life in the kingdom. Mark this: Unless you accept God's kingdom in the simplicity of a child, you'll never get in." Then, gathering the children up in his arms, he laid his hands of blessing on them.

Psalm 19:6 (MSG)
That's how God's Word vaults across the skies from sunrise to sunset, Melting ice, scorching deserts, warming hearts to faith.

Psalm 16:6 (ESV)
The lines have fallen for me in pleasant places; indeed, I have a beautiful inheritance.

Romans 5:2-5 (AMP)
Through Him we also have access by faith into this [remarkable state of] grace in which we [firmly and safely and securely] stand. Let us rejoice in our hope and the confident assurance of [experiencing and enjoying] the glory of [our great] God [the manifestation of His excellence and power]. 3 And not only this, but [with joy] let us exult in our sufferings and rejoice in our hardships, knowing that hardship (distress, pressure, trouble) produces patient endurance; 4 and endurance, proven character (spiritual maturity); and proven character, hope and confident assurance [of eternal salvation]. 5 Such hope [in God's promises] never disappoints us, because God's love has been abundantly poured out within our hearts through the Holy Spirit who was given to us.

My child,

Your life may feel out of control, but I can assure you that as you abide in my Spirit there will be no confusion or chaos. When you continually find yourself fighting with frustration, run to me. Take time to surrender everything to me. I want you to invite me into every area of your life. I am by your side, reach out and hold on to me. Trust me, I can handle this!

I Love You ~♥~

Isaiah 24:16-20 (MSG)
But I said, "That's all well and good for somebody, but all I can see is doom, doom, and more doom." All of them at one another's throats, yes, all of them at one another's throats. Terror and pits and booby traps are everywhere, whoever you are. If you run from the terror, you'll fall into the pit. If you climb out of the pit, you'll get caught in the trap. Chaos pours out of the skies. The foundations of earth are crumbling. Earth is smashed to pieces, earth is ripped to shreds, earth is wobbling out of control, Earth staggers like a drunk, sways like a shack in a high wind. Its piled-up sins are too much for it. It collapses and won't get up again.

1 Corinthians 9:1-3 (ESV)
Am I not free? Am I not an apostle? Have I not seen Jesus our Lord? Are not you my workmanship in the Lord? 2 If to others I am not an apostle, at least I am to you, for you are the seal of my apostleship in the Lord. 3 This is my defense to those who would examine me.

Isaiah 41:10 (NIV)
So do not fear, for I am with you; do not be dismayed, for I am your God. I will strengthen you and help you; I will uphold you with my righteous right hand.

Psalm 40:1-3 (NLT)
I waited patiently for the Lord to help me, and he turned to me and heard my cry. 2 He lifted me out of the pit of despair, out of the mud and the mire. He set my feet on solid ground and steadied me as I walked along. 3 He has given me a new song to sing, a hymn of praise to our God. Many will see what he has done and be amazed. They will put their trust in the Lord.

My child,

Often times you ask the question "what is my purpose?" I want to assure you and bring clarity to show you what you were created for. I made you with divine purpose and destiny. Search for me and find your true purpose. All things truly do work together. Don't get discouraged, keep pressing in - the answer will be revealed.

I Love You ~♥~

Jeremiah 29:11 (ESV)
For I know the plans I have for you, declares the Lord, plans for welfare and not for evil, to give you a future and a hope.

Psalm 139:23-24 (KJV)
Search me, O God, and know my heart: try me, and know my thoughts: 24 And see if there be any wicked way in me, and lead me in the way everlasting.

Matthew 7:7-11 (MSG)
"Don't bargain with God. Be direct. Ask for what you need. This isn't a cat-and-mouse, hide-and-seek game we're in. If your child asks for bread, do you trick him with sawdust? If he asks for fish, do you scare him with a live snake on his plate? As bad as you are, you wouldn't think of such a thing. You're at least decent to your own children. So don't you think the God who conceived you in love will be even better?"

Philippians 3:12-17 (NLT)
I don't mean to say that I have already achieved these things or that I have already reached perfection. But I press on to possess that perfection for which Christ Jesus first possessed me. 13 No, dear brothers and sisters, I have not achieved it, but I focus on this one thing: Forgetting the past and looking forward to what lies ahead, 14 I press on to reach the end of the race and receive the heavenly prize for which God, through Christ Jesus, is calling us. 15 Let all who are spiritually mature agree on these things. If you disagree on some point, I believe God will make it plain to you. 16 But we must hold on to the progress we have already made. 17 Dear brothers and sisters, pattern your lives after mine, and learn from those who follow our example.

My child,

I am aware of the turbulent times you have endured. Your emotions have been tossed to and fro. I want to remind you again, that you cannot find stability in mankind. I am your rock which you build upon - any other place will leave you sinking into an emotional pit. Why do you seek the living among what is dead? I have what you desire.

I Love You ~♥~

Ephesians 4:13-16 (ESV)
Until we all attain to the unity of the faith and of the knowledge of the Son of God, to mature manhood,to the measure of the stature of the fullness of Christ, 14 so that we may no longer be children, tossed to and fro by the waves and carried about by every wind of doctrine, by human cunning, by craftiness in deceitful schemes. 15 Rather, speaking the truth in love, we are to grow up in every way into him who is the head, into Christ, 16 from whom the whole body, joined and held together by every joint with which it is equipped, when each part is working properly, makes the body grow so that it builds itself up in love.

Matthew 7:24-27 (NLT)
"Anyone who listens to my teaching and follows it is wise, like a person who builds a house on solid rock. 25 Though the rain comes in torrents and the floodwaters rise and the winds beat against that house, it won't collapse because it is built on bedrock. 26 But anyone who hears my teaching and doesn't obey it is foolish, like a person who builds a house on sand. 27 When the rains and floods come and the winds beat against that house, it will collapse with a mighty crash."

Luke 24:5 (AMP)
...and as the women were terrified and were bowing their faces to the ground, the men said to them, "Why are you looking for the living One among the dead?"

Psalm 37:3-4 (MSG)
Get insurance with God and do a good deed, settle down and stick to your last. Keep company with God, get in on the best.

My Child,

I Love You

Be GRATEFUL Not Hateful

My child,

Fear forfeits my favor. I've called you to walk by faith. The enemy will try to trick you to become fearful and see things his way. By faith, resist him and he will flee. Walk in faith and find favor in me. I always have the answer waiting for you. Seek through faith and find me.

I Love You ~♥~

Proverbs 8:34-36 (ESV)
Blessed is the one who listens to me, watching daily at my gates, waiting beside my doors. 35 For whoever finds me finds life and obtains favor from the Lord, 36 but he who fails to find me injures himself; all who hate me love death."

Hebrews 3:12-14 (MSG)
So watch your step, friends. Make sure there's no evil unbelief lying around that will trip you up and throw you off course, diverting you from the living God. For as long as it's still God's Today, keep each other on your toes so sin doesn't slow down your reflexes. If we can only keep our grip on the sure thing we started out with, we're in this with Christ for the long haul. These words keep ringing in our ears: Today, please listen; don't turn a deaf ear as in the bitter uprising.

James 4:7 (ESV)
Submit yourselves therefore to God. Resist the devil, and he will flee from you.

Hebrews 11:6 (NLT)
And it is impossible to please God without faith. Anyone who wants to come to him must believe that God exists and that he rewards those who sincerely seek him.

My child,

Come away with me today. Put aside all other people, projects, preconceived notions and spend the day with me. Examine how you are spending your time. What are you investing in? Ask yourself, "does this have an eternal return?" Remember it is the enemy that comes to steal and he will rob you of your time with me. I miss you.

I Love You ~♥~

Psalm 55:16-17 (KJV)
As for me, I will call upon God; and the Lord shall save me. 17 Evening, and morning, and at noon, will I pray, and cry aloud: and he shall hear my voice.

Ecclesiastes 3:11 (ESV)
He has made everything beautiful in its time. Also, he has put eternity into man's heart, yet so that he cannot find out what God has done from the beginning to the end.

2 Corinthians 4:16-18 (MSG)
So we're not giving up. How could we! Even though on the outside it often looks like things are falling apart on us, on the inside, where God is making new life, not a day goes by without his unfolding grace. These hard times are small potatoes compared to the coming good times, the lavish celebration prepared for us. There's far more here than meets the eye. The things we see now are here today, gone tomorrow. But the things we can't see now will last forever.

Ephesians 5:15-17 (NLT)
So be careful how you live. Don't live like fools, but like those who are wise. 16 Make the most of every opportunity in these evil days. 17 Don't act thoughtlessly, but understand what the Lord wants you to do.

John 10:10 (AMP)
The thief comes only in order to steal and kill and destroy. I came that they may have and enjoy life, and have it in abundance [to the full, till it overflows].

My child,
Put first things first. I must be first in your life. As you make adjustments to realign yourself with me, I will show you areas where you spend too much unproductive time. When you put me first I will partner in everything you do, and our work will be more productive throughout the day and for my Kingdom.

I Love You ~♥~

Exodus 20:3 (KJV)
Thou shalt have no other gods before me.

2 Corinthians 8:5-7 (ESV)
...and this, not as we expected, but they gave themselves first to the Lord and then by the will of God to us. 6 Accordingly, we urged Titus that as he had started, so he should complete among you this act of grace. 7 But as you excel in everything—in faith, in speech, in knowledge, in all earnestness, and in our love for you—see that you excel in this act of grace also.

Romans 12:1-2 (MSG)
So here's what I want you to do, God helping you: Take your everyday, ordinary life—your sleeping, eating, going-to-work, and walking-around life—and place it before God as an offering. Embracing what God does for you is the best thing you can do for him. Don't become so well-adjusted to your culture that you fit into it without even thinking. Instead, fix your attention on God. You'll be changed from the inside out. Readily recognize what he wants from you, and quickly respond to it. Unlike the culture around you, always dragging you down to its level of immaturity, God brings the best out of you, develops well-formed maturity in you.

Philippians 4:13 (AMP)
I can do all things [which He has called me to do] through Him who strengthens and empowers me [to fulfill His purpose—I am self-sufficient in Christ's sufficiency; I am ready for anything and equal to anything through Him who infuses me with inner strength and confident peace.]

My child,

Why do you look to man for your validation? I know your name. Don't put your confidence in man. I am God, your God. I tell the sun when to rise and to set. Why don't you believe that I can order your steps? When you become anxious over man-made problems, it puts a stumbling block in front of your faith! Walk with me and trust me to lead you.

I Love You ~♥~

Psalm 118:8 (KJV)
It is better to trust in the Lord than to put confidence in man.

1 Corinthians 10:14 (MSG)
So, my very dear friends, when you see people reducing God to something they can use or control, get out of their company as fast as you can.

Psalm 113:3 (NIV)
From the rising of the sun to the place where it sets, the name of the Lord is to be praised.

Matthew 16:23 (AMP)
But Jesus turned and said to Peter, "Get behind Me, Satan! You are a stumbling block to Me; for you are not setting your mind on things of God, but on things of man."

My child,

I am the God of new beginnings. Every day is an opportunity for new avenues, adventures and attitudes. You must choose to acknowledge and
accept the "new" I'm bringing to your life. Abide in me for I am with you.

I Love You ~♥~

Ecclesiastes 3:11 (AMP)
He has made everything beautiful and appropriate in its time. He has also planted eternity [a sense of divine purpose] in the human heart [a mysterious longing which nothing under the sun can satisfy, except God]—yet man cannot find out (comprehend, grasp) what God has done (His overall plan) from the beginning to the end.

Ezekiel 36:26 (ESV)
And I will give you a new heart, and a new spirit I will put within you. And I will remove the heart of stone from your flesh and give you a heart of flesh.

Ephesians 4:22-24 (HCSB)
You took off your former way of life, the old self that is corrupted by deceitful desires; 23 you are being renewed in the spirit of your minds; 24 you put on the new self, the one created according to God's likeness in righteousness and purity of the truth.

Lamentations 3:22-24 (MSG)
God's loyal love couldn't have run out, his merciful love couldn't have dried up. They're created new every morning. How great your faithfulness! I'm sticking with God (I say it over and over). He's all I've got left.

1 John 2:27-28 (NLT)
But you have received the Holy Spirit, and he lives within you, so you don't need anyone to teach you what is true. For the Spirit teaches you everything you need to know, and what he teaches is true—it is not a lie. So just as he has taught you, remain in fellowship with Christ. 28 And now, dear children, remain in fellowship with Christ so that when he returns, you will be full of courage and not shrink back from him in shame.

My Child,

_____

I Love You

Stay in Alignment with Your Assignment

My child,

Look around - do you see what I see? When sickness comes, do you see destruction or even death? I see an opportunity to show I am the God that heals. When negative words are spoken over your life, do you agree with them? I want you to believe my words and see yourself as a reflection of me. When wounds from your past still are hurting, do you see yourself staying bound? I see the blood of Jesus covering your hurts and setting you free - forever! Look through my eyes, your vision will change.

I Love You ~♥~

Romans 6:8-10 (ESV)
Now if we have died with Christ, we believe that we will also live with him. 9 We know that Christ, being raised from the dead, will never die again; death no longer has dominion over him. 10 For the death he died he died to sin, once for all, but the life he lives he lives to God.

Exodus 15:26 (AMP)
saying, "If you will diligently listen and pay attention to the voice of the Lord your God, and do what is right in His sight, and listen to His commandments, and keep [foremost in your thoughts and actively obey] all His precepts and statutes, then I will not put on you any of the diseases which I have put on the Egyptians; for I am the Lord who heals you."

2 Timothy 3:1-5 (MSG)
Don't be naive. There are difficult times ahead. As the end approaches, people are going to be self-absorbed, money-hungry, self-promoting, stuck-up, profane, contemptuous of parents, crude, coarse, dog-eat-dog, unbending, slanderers, impulsively wild, savage, cynical, treacherous, ruthless, bloated windbags, addicted to lust, and allergic to God. They'll make a show of religion, but behind the scenes they're animals. Stay clear of these people.

2 Corinthians 3:17-18 (ISV)
Now the Lord is the Spirit, and where the Lord's Spirit is, there is freedom. 18 As all of us reflect the glory of the Lord with unveiled faces, we are becoming more like him with ever-increasing glory by the Lord's Spirit.

My child,

Do you need to hit the reset button? There is a way for you to reunite with me. Repent, renounce, and reconcile with me. I am not your enemy. I do not want to hurt or harm you. I will redirect your steps, but you must decide to walk with me. Set your mind - never to return to the old dead things again. Your life will be filled with blessings and joy in my presence.

I Love You ~♥~

Job 36:5-15 (MSG)
"It's true that God is all-powerful, but he doesn't bully innocent people. For the wicked, though, it's a different story— he doesn't give them the time of day, but champions the rights of their victims. He never takes his eyes off the righteous; he honors them lavishly, promotes them endlessly. When things go badly, when affliction and suffering descend, God tells them where they've gone wrong, shows them how their pride has caused their trouble. He forces them to heed his warning, tells them they must repent of their bad life. If they obey and serve him, they'll have a good, long life on easy street. But if they disobey, they'll be cut down in their prime and never know the first thing about life. Angry people without God pile grievance upon grievance, always blaming others for their troubles. Living it up in sexual excesses, virility wasted, they die young. But those who learn from their suffering, God delivers from their suffering."

2 Corinthians 5:20 (ESV)
Therefore, we are ambassadors for Christ, God making his appeal through us. We implore you on behalf of Christ, be reconciled to God.

Job 11:13-15 (HCSB)
As for you, if you redirect your heart and lift up your hands to Him in prayer - 14 if there is iniquity in your hand, remove it, and don't allow injustice to dwell in your tents - 15 then you will hold your head high, free from fault. You will be firmly established and unafraid.

Deuteronomy 28:2 (KJV)
And all these blessings shall come on thee, and overtake thee, if thou shalt hearken unto the voice of the Lord thy God.

My child,

Let your words be few today. Open your ears to hear me speaking to you. Seek to know me and my heart for you. I am the best friend you'll ever have or need. Intimacy with me means you can share your true feelings with me. You are important to me.

I Love You ~♥~

Ecclesiastes 5:2 (ESV)
Be not rash with your mouth, nor let your heart be hasty to utter a word before God, for God is in heaven and you are on earth. Therefore let your words be few.

John 15:13-14 (AMP)
No one has greater love [nor stronger commitment] than to lay down his own life for his friends. 14 You are my friends if you keep on doing what I command you.

1 Corinthians 10:31-33 (MSG)
So eat your meals heartily, not worrying about what others say about you—you're eating to God's glory, after all, not to please them. As a matter of fact, do everything that way, heartily and freely to God's glory. At the same time, don't be callous in your exercise of freedom, thoughtlessly stepping on the toes of those who aren't as free as you are. I try my best to be considerate of everyone's feelings in all these matters; I hope you will be, too.

My child,

Long before you were in existence I had thoughts of you. And to this day you are in my thoughts. Never doubt my care or concern for you. You are my beloved and what comes to your life I will deliver throughout your life. Keep believing my words, living in my will and I'll show you the way.

I Love You ~♥~

Jeremiah 1:5 (MSG)
"Before I shaped you in the womb, I knew all about you. Before you saw the light of day, I had holy plans for you: A prophet to the nations— that's what I had in mind for you."

Psalm 40:5 (ESV)
You have multiplied, O Lord my God, your wondrous deeds and your thoughts toward us; none can compare with you! I will proclaim and tell of them, yet they are more than can be told.

Ecclesiastes 11:5 (HCSB)
Just as you don't know the path of the wind, or how bones develop in the womb of a pregnant woman, so you don't know the work of God who makes everything.

John 20:31 (AMP)
but these have been written so that you may believe [with a deep, abiding trust] that Jesus is the Christ (the Messiah, the Anointed), the Son of God; and that by believing [and trusting in and relying on Him] you may have life in His name.

My child,

I am aware that you have been experiencing oppressing spirits coming against you. But, I say, "Fear not, I have called you to be more than conquerors through me." Rise up and take authority over those tormenting vile spirits. They must bow to my name. You are victorious!

I Love You ~♥~

1 Peter 5:8-11 (AMP)
Be sober [well balanced and self-disciplined], be alert and cautious at all times. That enemy of yours, the devil, prowls around like a roaring lion [fiercely hungry], seeking someone to devour. 9 But resist him, be firm in your faith [against his attack—rooted, established, immovable], knowing that the same experiences of suffering are being experienced by your brothers and sisters throughout the world. [You do not suffer alone.] 10 After you have suffered for a little while, the God of all grace [who imparts His blessing and favor], who called you to His own eternal glory in Christ, will Himself complete, confirm, strengthen, and establish you [making you what you ought to be]. 11 To Him be dominion (power, authority, sovereignty) forever and ever. Amen.

1 John 4:4-6 (MSG)
My dear children, you come from God and belong to God. You have already won a big victory over those false teachers, for the Spirit in you is far stronger than anything in the world. These people belong to the Christ-denying world. They talk the world's language and the world eats it up. But we come from God and belong to God. Anyone who knows God understands us and listens. The person who has nothing to do with God will, of course, not listen to us. This is another test for telling the Spirit of Truth from the spirit of deception.

My Child,

_____

_____

_____

_____

_____

_____

_____

_____

_____

_____

_____

_____

_____

_____

_____

_____

_____

_____

_____

_____

_____

_____

_____

_____

_____

_____

I Love You

~ ~

the seed you're sowing is growing

My child,

You speak of wanting freedom, but you must recognize the areas in your life where you are choosing to stay bound. I came to set you free; my desire for you is complete freedom. However, you must relinquish all your rights to me in every area of your life. Today, if you will ask me if you are holding anything back - I will reveal it. When you let go, you will find freedom!

I Love You ~♥~

2 Peter 2:19 (ESV)
They promise them freedom, but they themselves are slaves of corruption. For whatever overcomes a person, to that he is enslaved.

Galatians 5:1 (AMP)
It was for this freedom that Christ set us free [completely liberating us]; therefore keep standing firm and do not be subject again to a yoke of slavery [which you once removed].

1 Corinthians 9:12 (HCSB)
If others have this right to receive benefits from you, don't we even more? However, we have not made use of this right; instead we endure everything so that we will not hinder the gospel of Christ.

Romans 8:21 (NLT)
...the creation looks forward to the day when it will join God's children in glorious freedom from death and decay.

My child,

Even when you're walking through a valley, I am with you. The valleys of life are preparing you for the mountaintop. When you find yourself in the struggle of the valley, lift up your head and praise me for the victory I am sending. You are not stuck in this place - find grace and move on to the mountaintop with me.

I Love You ~♥~

Psalm 23:4 (ESV)
Even though I walk through the valley of the shadow of death, I will fear no evil, for you are with me; your rod and your staff, they comfort me.

Exodus 19:20 (AMP)
The Lord came down on Mount Sinai, to the top of the mountain; and the Lord called Moses to the top of the mountain, and he went up.

Luke 22:27-30 (MSG)
"Who would you rather be: the one who eats the dinner or the one who serves the dinner? You'd rather eat and be served, right? But I've taken my place among you as the one who serves. And you've stuck with me through thick and thin. Now I confer on you the royal authority my Father conferred on me so you can eat and drink at my table in my kingdom and be strengthened as you take up responsibilities among the congregations of God's people."

Acts 20:32 (NLT)
"And now I entrust you to God and the message of his grace that is able to build you up and give you an inheritance with all those he has set apart for himself."

My child,

It is time for you to enjoy your journey through life. There will be obstacles and opportunities on your journey. You have the choice to make; live in fear or walk by faith. Fear paralyzes you and stops you from living the life I destined you to live. Choosing faith brings freedom and favor to your life. Your faith shows you trust me.

I Love You ~♥~

Judges 18:5-6 (HCSB)
Then they said to him, "Please inquire of God so we will know if we will have a successful journey." 6 The priest told them, "Go in peace. The Lord is watching over the journey you are going on."

1 Timothy 6:12 (AMP)
Fight the good fight of the faith [in the conflict with evil]; take hold of the eternal life to which you were called, and [for which] you made the good confession [of faith] in the presence of many witnesses.

Hebrews 12:2 (KJV)
Looking unto Jesus the author and finisher of our faith; who for the joy that was set before him endured the cross, despising the shame, and is set down at the right hand of the throne of God.

Philippians 1:6 (NIV)
...being confident of this, that he who began a good work in you will carry it on to completion until the day of Christ Jesus.

Jeremiah 17:7-8 (NLT)
"But blessed are those who trust in the Lord and have made the Lord their hope and confidence. 8 They are like trees planted along a riverbank, with roots that reach deep into the water. Such trees are not bothered by the heat or worried by long months of drought. Their leaves stay green, and they never stop producing fruit.

My child,

Often times when you are backed into a corner with nowhere else to go, you experience a deeper intimacy with me. In times such as these, I can show my strength, power and deliverance through your life. It is better to embrace the hard place because that is where the bigger blessing will be found. As we face this together, our relationship will be fortified.

I Love You ~♥~

Psalm 22:27-28 (MSG)
From the four corners of the earth people are coming to their senses, are running back to God. Long-lost families are falling on their faces before him. God has taken charge; from now on he has the last word.

Psalm 119:25-32 (MSG)
I'm feeling terrible—I couldn't feel worse! Get me on my feet again. You promised, remember? When I told my story, you responded; train me well in your deep wisdom. Help me understand these things inside and out so I can ponder your miracle-wonders. My sad life's dilapidated, a falling-down barn; build me up again by your Word. Barricade the road that goes Nowhere; grace me with your clear revelation. I choose the true road to Somewhere, I post your road signs at every curve and corner. I grasp and cling to whatever you tell me; God, don't let me down! I'll run the course you lay out for me if you'll just show me how.

1 Corinthians 1:25 (NLT)
This foolish plan of God is wiser than the wisest of human plans, and God's weakness is stronger than the greatest of human strength.

My child,

When you release your life to me, you will truly begin to live. I am in control. If you could look through the eyes that I gave you, your vision will change. No longer will you see man, but you'll see me. I'll show you my power to protect and perfect you. Don't run from the roar; it's only noise- it has no authority over you.

I Love You ~♥~

Matthew 10:39 (NLT)
If you cling to your life, you will lose it; but if you give up your life for me, you will find it.

Psalm 141:8-9 (ESV)
But my eyes are toward you, O God, my Lord; in you I seek refuge; leave me not defenseless! 9 Keep me from the trap that they have laid for me and from the snares of evildoers!

1 John 5:18 (AMP)
We know [with confidence] that anyone born of God does not habitually sin; but He (Jesus) who was born of God [carefully] keeps and protects him, and the evil one does not touch him.

Hebrews 12:2 (NASB)
...fixing our eyes on Jesus, the author and perfecter of faith, who for the joy set before Him endured the cross, despising the shame, and has sat down at the right hand of the throne of God.

1 Peter 5:8-11 (MSG)
Keep a cool head. Stay alert. The Devil is poised to pounce, and would like nothing better than to catch you napping. Keep your guard up. You're not the only ones plunged into these hard times. It's the same with Christians all over the world. So keep a firm grip on the faith. The suffering won't last forever. It won't be long before this generous God who has great plans for us in Christ—eternal and glorious plans they are!—will have you put together and on your feet for good. He gets the last word; yes, he does.

My Child,

I Love You

complain & remain GIVE praise AND raise

My child,

As you go through your life, you are given opportunities to witness to others. The enemy is working diligently to increase hell. You are called to enlarge my Kingdom. Will you take time to share and show the gospel with lost people? Look around you - who do you see that needs me? Well, then today tell them about me. They will be glad you loved them enough to spare them.

I Love You ~♥~

Psalm 96:2-4 (KJV)
Sing unto the Lord, bless his name; shew forth his salvation from day to day. 3 Declare his glory among the heathen, his wonders among all people. 4 For the Lord is great, and greatly to be praised: he is to be feared above all gods.

John 10:10 (ESV)
The thief comes only to steal and kill and destroy. I came that they may have life and have it abundantly.

Matthew 28:18-20 (MSG)
Jesus, undeterred, went right ahead and gave his charge: "God authorized and commanded me to commission you: Go out and train everyone you meet, far and near, in this way of life, marking them by baptism in the threefold name: Father, Son, and Holy Spirit. Then instruct them in the practice of all I have commanded you. I'll be with you as you do this, day after day after day, right up to the end of the age."

My child,

Do not compromise your testimony of faith. There are many eyes watching you, trying to see if you are different from the world. I am calling you to put off the worldliness and clothe yourself with the word. Do not fear rejection of man. Do not fall away from following my ways. Let your light shine brightly to guide others to me.

I Love You ~♥~

1 Timothy 4:12 (ESV)
Let no one despise you for your youth, but set the believers an example in speech, in conduct, in love, in faith, in purity.

Philippians 3:17-18 (HCSB)
Join in imitating me, brothers, and observe those who live according to the example you have in us. 18 For I have often told you, and now say again with tears, that many live as enemies of the cross of Christ.

Titus 2:11-13 (KJV)
For the grace of God that bringeth salvation hath appeared to all men, 12 Teaching us that, denying ungodliness and worldly lusts, we should live soberly, righteously, and godly, in this present world; 13 Looking for that blessed hope, and the glorious appearing of the great God and our Saviour Jesus Christ;

1 Peter 1:13-14 (NIV)
Therefore, with minds that are alert and fully sober, set your hope on the grace to be brought to you when Jesus Christ is revealed at his coming. 14 As obedient children, do not conform to the evil desires you had when you lived in ignorance.

Romans 13:13 (NLT)
Because we belong to the day, we must live decent lives for all to see. Don't participate in the darkness of wild parties and drunkenness, or in sexual promiscuity and immoral living, or in quarreling and jealousy.

My child,

Listen to me. I need you to focus and give me your full attention. As of late, you have been distracted to the point that it's bringing division to your heart. That disgruntled feeling you are dealing with is the enemy of your soul - he will never stop trying to deceive you. You must realize the truth by recognizing the true enemy. Look only to me for deliverance and dedicate your whole heart to me.

I Love You ~♥~

Psalm 123:2 (AMP)
Behold, as the eyes of servants look to the hand of their master, And as the eyes of a maid to the hand of her mistress, so our eyes look to the Lord our God, Until He is gracious and favorable toward us.

Isaiah 28:23 (ESV)
Give ear, and hear my voice; give attention, and hear my speech.

Hosea 10:2 (KJV)
Their heart is divided; now shall they be found faulty: he shall break down their altars, he shall spoil their images.

Psalm 143:3-6 (NLT)
My enemy has chased me. He has knocked me to the ground and forces me to live in darkness like those in the grave. 4 I am losing all hope; I am paralyzed with fear. 5 I remember the days of old. I ponder all your great works and think about what you have done. 6 I lift my hands to you in prayer. I thirst for you as parched land thirsts for rain.

Hebrews 2:1-4 (MSG)
It's crucial that we keep a firm grip on what we've heard so that we don't drift off. If the old message delivered by the angels was valid and nobody got away with anything, do you think we can risk neglecting this latest message, this magnificent salvation? First of all, it was delivered in person by the Master, then accurately passed on to us by those who heard it from him. All the while God was validating it with gifts through the Holy Spirit, all sorts of signs and miracles, as he saw fit.

My child,

Your love for me is contagious. When others see your trust in me, they want what you have. You are leading others to me through love. My love will never fail you or others around you. Hold fast to my everlasting, never wavering, constant and pure love. You are a vessel for my love - let me flow through you.

I Love You ~♥~

1 Corinthians:3-10 (MSG)
If I give everything I own to the poor and even go to the stake to be burned as a martyr, but I don't love, I've gotten nowhere. So, no matter what I say, what I believe, and what I do, I'm bankrupt without love. Love never gives up. Love cares more for others than for self.
Love doesn't want what it doesn't have.
Love doesn't strut,
Doesn't have a swelled head,
Doesn't force itself on others,
Isn't always "me first,"
Doesn't fly off the handle,
Doesn't keep score of the sins of others,
Doesn't revel when others grovel,
Takes pleasure in the flowering of truth,
Puts up with anything,
Trusts God always, Always looks for the best,
Never looks back, But keeps going to the end.
Love never dies. Inspired speech will be over some day; praying in tongues will end; understanding will reach its limit. We know only a portion of the truth, and what we say about God is always incomplete. But when the Complete arrives, our incompletes will be canceled.

1 Peter 4:8 (ESV)
Above all, keep loving one another earnestly, since love covers a multitude of sins.

My child,

You are valuable. Your life is valuable. It's not your possessions that make you rich, but your relationship with me and others. How are you investing your time, talents, treasures and temple? I want you to understand the blood of Jesus invested into your life was not cheap. I am asking you to use the investment made in you, to invest in others. Make sure those around you know me. Take time to invest yourself in others. I guarantee a great return!

I Love You ~♥~

1 Corinthians 7:23-24 (MSG)
All of you, slave and free both, were once held hostage in a sinful society. Then a huge sum was paid out for your ransom. So please don't, out of old habit, slip back into being or doing what everyone else tells you. Friends, stay where you were called to be. God is there. Hold the high ground with him at your side.

Matthew 6:20-21 (AMP)
But store up for yourselves treasures in heaven, where neither moth nor rust destroys, and where thieves do not break in and steal; 21 for where your treasure is, there your heart [your wishes, your desires; that on which your life centers] will be also.

Philippians 3:8 (ESV)
Indeed, I count everything as loss because of the surpassing worth of knowing Christ Jesus my Lord. For his sake I have suffered the loss of all things and count them as rubbish, in order that I may gain Christ.

John 3:16 (KJV)
For God so loved the world, that he gave his only begotten Son, that whosoever believeth in him should not perish, but have everlasting life.

1 Peter 1:19-21 (NLT)
It was the precious blood of Christ, the sinless, spotless Lamb of God. 20 God chose him as your ransom long before the world began, but now in these last days he has been revealed for your sake. 21 Through Christ you have come to trust in God. And you have placed your faith and hope in God because he raised Christ from the dead and gave him great glory.

My Child,

I Love You

My child,

Where does your hope come from? Are you placing hope in man-made methods? If so, you will be disappointed and disillusioned by man. I am the answer to hope. You can hope in me. It is a blessing to me to watch you hope against the odds. This allows my power to show forth in your situations of life. Stay hope-filled in me and me alone. I will not disappoint you!

I Love You ~♥~

Psalm 31:24 (KJV)
Be of good courage, and he shall strengthen your heart, all ye that hope in the Lord.

Ephesians 3:20-21 (AMP)
Now to Him who is able to [carry out His purpose and] do superabundantly more than all that we dare ask or think [infinitely beyond our greatest prayers, hopes, or dreams], according to His power that is at work within us, 21 to Him be the glory in the church and in Christ Jesus throughout all generations forever and ever. Amen.

Romans 12:12 (NLT)
Rejoice in our confident hope. Be patient in trouble, and keep on praying.

Colossians 1:27 (HCSB)
God wanted to make known among the Gentiles the glorious wealth of this mystery, which is Christ in you, the hope of glory.

My child,
You are in the world but worldliness does not have to be in you. Take time and examine your heart. Have you been affecting the world or has the world be infecting you? I have called you to higher ground, to live above your circumstances. You have a greater power through me to overcome and impact those around you for my kingdom. Rise up and walk the narrow path. You are worthy of this calling.

I Love You ~♥~

1 John 2:15-17 (NLT)
Do not love this world nor the things it offers you, for when you love the world, you do not have the love of the Father in you. For the world offers only a craving for physical pleasure, a craving for everything we see, and pride in our achievements and possessions. These are not from the Father, but are from this world. And this world is fading away, along with everything that people crave. But anyone who does what pleases God will live forever.

John 17:16-17 (KJV)
They are not of the world, even as I am not of the world. 17 Sanctify them through thy truth: thy word is truth.

John 15:19 (AMP)
If you belonged to the world, the world would love [you as] its own and would treat you with affection. But you are not of the world [you no longer belong to it], but I have chosen you out of the world. And because of this the world hates you.

1 John 4:4 (ESV)
Little children, you are from God and have overcome them, for he who is in you is greater than he who is in the world.

My child,

Today I want you to release everything to me. Release your fear and I'll replace it with faith. Release your bitterness and I'll replace it with blessings. Release unforgiveness and I'll replace it with unity. Release anger and I'll replace it with anticipation. The choice is yours to make. You will not be empty for I will replace that space.

I Love You ~♥~

Ephesians 3:12 (ERV)
In Christ we come before God with freedom and without fear. We can do this because of our faith in Christ.

Ephesians 4:31-32 (KJV)
Let all bitterness, and wrath, and anger, and clamour, and evil speaking, be put away from you, with all malice: 32 And be ye kind one to another, tenderhearted, forgiving one another, even as God for Christ's sake hath forgiven you.

Ephesians 1:3-5 (AMP)
Blessed and worthy of praise be the God and Father of our Lord Jesus Christ, who has blessed us with every spiritual blessing in the heavenly realms in Christ, 4 just as [in His love] He chose us in Christ [actually selected us for Himself as His own] before the foundation of the world, so that we would be holy [that is, consecrated, set apart for Him, purpose-driven] and blameless in His sight. In love 5 He predestined and lovingly planned for us to be adopted to Himself as [His own] children through Jesus Christ, in accordance with the kind intention and good pleasure of His will—

Zechariah 9:11-13 (MSG)
"And you, because of my blood covenant with you, I'll release your prisoners from their hopeless cells. Come home, hope-filled prisoners! This very day I'm declaring a double bonus— everything you lost returned twice-over! Judah is now my weapon, the bow I'll pull, setting Ephraim as an arrow to the string. I'll wake up your sons, O Zion, to counter your sons, O Greece. From now on people are my swords."

My child,

I see that you are struggling with performance. I want you to know this down in your heart - You are enough! The world places unnecessary pressure on you to strive for more, but I call you to abide and find everything in me. You are free from measuring yourself by man's standards. Align yourself with me and you will find freedom like you have never known. Life is more about who you are in me than what you have in the world.

I Love You ~♥~

Psalm 51:16-17 (MSG)
Going through the motions doesn't please you, a flawless performance is nothing to you. I learned God-worship when my pride was shattered. Heart-shattered lives ready for love don't for a moment escape God's notice.

Matthew 6:1 (HCSB)
Be careful not to practice your righteousness in front of people, to be seen by them. Otherwise, you will have no reward from your Father in heaven.

1 John 4:12-16 (AMP)
No one has seen God at any time. But if we love one another [with unselfish concern], God abides in us, and His love [the love that is His essence abides in us and] is completed and perfected in us. 13 By this we know [with confident assurance] that we abide in Him and He in us, because He has given to us His [Holy] Spirit. 14 We [who were with Him in person] have seen and testify [as eye-witnesses] that the Father has sent the Son to be the Savior of the world. 15 Whoever confesses and acknowledges that Jesus is the Son of God, God abides in him, and he in God. 16 We have come to know [by personal observation and experience], and have believed [with deep, consistent faith] the love which God has for us. God is love, and the one who abides in love abides in God, and God abides continually in him.

My child,

I know you struggle with regrets over the past. While it is true you cannot change the past, you can change how you view your past. Instead of looking back at all the hurts from the past, see my healing in the present. To be victorious over your past, learn from it and live differently. I've called you to new life in me. Your old self is gone, behold you are new.

I Love You ~❤~

2 Corinthians 7:10(MSG)
Distress that drives us to God does that. It turns us around. It gets us back in the way of salvation. We never regret that kind of pain. But those who let distress drive them away from God are full of regrets, end up on a deathbed of regrets.

Psalm 34:4-5 (ESV)
I sought the Lord, and he answered me and delivered me from all my fears. 5 Those who look to him are radiant, and their faces shall never be ashamed.

Isaiah 43:18-19 (KJV)
Remember ye not the former things, neither consider the things of old. 19 Behold, I will do a new thing; now it shall spring forth; shall ye not know it? I will even make a way in the wilderness, and rivers in the desert.

2 Peter 1:8-9 (NLT)
The more you grow like this, the more productive and useful you will be in your knowledge of our Lord Jesus Christ. 9 But those who fail to develop in this way are shortsighted or blind, forgetting that they have been cleansed from their old sins

My Child,

I Love You

My child,

You can continually dwell in my presence: If daily you choose to crucify the flesh, forgive those who offend you and follow me with your whole heart. You must surrender every area to me and trust me to take care of you. I created you to worship me - don't allow anything or anyone to stand in the way of your worship.

I Love You ~♥~

Jude 24-25 (NIV)
To him who is able to keep you from stumbling and to present you before his glorious presence without fault and with great joy - 25 to the only God our Savior be glory, majesty, power and authority, through Jesus Christ our Lord, before all ages, now and forevermore! Amen.

Acts 3:19-21 (ESV)
Repent therefore, and turn back, that your sins may be blotted out, 20 that times of refreshing may come from the presence of the Lord, and that he may send the Christ appointed for you, Jesus, 21 whom heaven must receive until the time for restoring all the things about which God spoke by the mouth of his holy prophets long ago.

Job 11:13-15 (CEV)
Surrender your heart to God, turn to him in prayer, 14 and give up your sins - even those you do in secret. 15 Then you won't be ashamed; you will be confident and fearless.

John 4:23-24 (NKJV)
"But the hour is coming, and now is, when the true worshipers will worship the Father in spirit and truth; for the Father is seeking such to worship Him. 24 God is Spirit, and those who worship Him must worship in spirit and truth."

Revelation 4:11 (AMP)
"Worthy are You, our Lord and God, to receive the glory and the honor and the power; for You created all things, and because of Your will they exist, and were created and brought into being."

My child,

It is time for you to embrace how valuable you are to me. You live in a world where people are easily replaced, discarded and/or devalued. Your worth will never come into question in my kingdom. I created you for greatness; nothing less. I proclaim you are worthy!

I Love you ~♥~

Matthew 10:31 (ESV)
Fear not, therefore; you are of more value than many sparrows.

Psalm 139:13-16 (AMP)
For You formed my innermost parts; You knit me [together] in my mother's womb. 14 I will give thanks and praise to You, for I am fearfully and wonderfully made; Wonderful are Your works, And my soul knows it very well. 15 My frame was not hidden from You, When I was being formed in secret, And intricately and skillfully formed [as if embroidered with many colors] in the depths of the earth.16 Your eyes have seen my unformed substance; And in Your book were all written The days that were appointed for me, When as yet there was not one of them [even taking shape].

Matthew 6:26 (HCSB)
Look at the birds of the sky: They don't sow or reap or gather into barns, yet your heavenly Father feeds them. Aren't you worth more than they?

1 Peter 2:9-10 (MSG)
But you are the ones chosen by God, chosen for the high calling of priestly work, chosen to be a holy people, God's instruments to do his work and speak out for him, to tell others of the night-and-day difference he made for you—from nothing to something, from rejected to accepted.

My child,

You have been called out of the darkness. Why are you still lingering in dark places? You have been delivered and set free. You will find nothing of value in the darkness. It will only cost you - stop it now before it consumes you again. Step into my marvelous light and live free and full of me!

I Love You ~♥~

Colossians 1:13-14 (MSG)
God rescued us from dead-end alleys and dark dungeons. He's set us up in the kingdom of the Son he loves so much, the Son who got us out of the pit we were in, got rid of the sins we were doomed to keep repeating.

Psalm 107:14 (AMP)
He brought them out of darkness and the deep (deathly) darkness
And broke their bonds apart.

Ephesians 5:8-10 (ESV)
for at one time you were darkness, but now you are light in the Lord. Walk as children of light 9 (for the fruit of light is found in all that is good and right and true), 10 and try to discern what is pleasing to the Lord.

John 8:12 (NLT)
Jesus spoke to the people once more and said, "I am the light of the world. If you follow me, you won't have to walk in darkness, because you will have the light that leads to life."

My child,

Before you can understand my ways, you must first understand my word. You will not stand strong unless you study my word – this book has stood the test of time and won! The words are alive and active. You will be amazed at the wonderful journey it will take you on. Open the Bible, jump in and dive deep into my word. Get to know me better – You'll be glad you did, and so will I!

I Love You ~♥~

Psalm 25:9 (HCSB)
He leads the humble in what is right and teaches them His way.

John 14:5-7 (MSG)
Thomas said, "Master, we have no idea where you're going. How do you expect us to know the road?" Jesus said, "I am the Road, also the Truth, also the Life. No one gets to the Father apart from me. If you really knew me, you would know my Father as well. From now on, you do know him. You've even seen him!"

Psalm 86:11 (NLT)
Teach me your ways, O Lord, that I may live according to your truth! Grant me purity of heart, so that I may honor you.

1 Corinthians 16:13 (ESV)
Be watchful, stand firm in the faith, act like men, be strong.

Philippians 1:27 (AMP)
Only [be sure to] lead your lives in a manner [that will be] worthy of the gospel of Christ, so that whether I do come and see you or remain absent, I will hear about you that you are standing firm in one spirit [and one purpose], with one mind striving side by side [as if in combat] for the faith of the gospel.

My child,
Today you can choose to look to man or look to me. You will never find in man what I can give you. I see you searching to the point of exhaustion and I know it's an unnecessary plight in life for you. When you stay in my will for your life, I make a way for you to live. No man can do that for you!

I Love You ~♥~

1 Chronicles 16:11 (AMP)
Seek the Lord and His strength; Seek His face continually [longing to be in His presence].

Psalm 14:2 (ESV)
The Lord looks down from heaven on the children of man, to see if there are any who understand, who seek after God.

Deuteronomy 4:29-31 (HCSB)
But from there, you will search for the Lord your God, and you will find Him when you seek Him with all your heart and all your soul. 30 When you are in distress and all these things have happened to you, you will return to the Lord your God in later days and obey Him. 31 He will not leave you, destroy you, or forget the covenant with your fathers that He swore to them by oath, because the Lord your God is a compassionate God.

Luke 12:31 (NLT)
Seek the Kingdom of God above all else, and he will give you everything you need.

Isaiah 43:16-19 (NIV)
This is what the Lord says— he who made a way through the sea, a path through the mighty waters, 17 who drew out the chariots and horses, the army and reinforcements together, and they lay there, never to rise again, extinguished, snuffed out like a wick: 18 "Forget the former things; do not dwell on the past. 19 See, I am doing a new thing! Now it springs up; do you not perceive it? I am making a way in the wilderness and streams in the wasteland."

My Child,

I Love You

~ ~

RELEASE
so you can have
PEACE

My child,

It's time to activate your faith. Today, whatever circumstances, obstacles or problems you encounter, I want you to shout, "My GOD is bigger!"
I AM the GREAT I AM! The desire of my heart is to show you how in control and connected I AM in your life.

I Love You ~♥~

1 Peter 1:8-9 (ESV)
Though you have not seen him, you love him. Though you do not now see him, you believe in him and rejoice with joy that is inexpressible and filled with glory, 9 obtaining the outcome of your faith, the salvation of your souls.

John 11:40 (AMP)
Jesus said to her, "Did I not say to you that if you believe [in Me], you will see the glory of God [the expression of His excellence]?"

James 2:17 (NLT)
So you see, faith by itself isn't enough. Unless it produces good deeds, it is dead and useless.

John 6:35 (NIV)
Jesus said to them, "I am the bread of life; he who comes to Me will not hunger, and he who believes in Me will never thirst."

John 8:23 (NIV)
And He was saying to them, "You are from below, I am from above; you are of this world, I am not of this world.

John 10:7 (NIV)
So Jesus said to them again, "Truly, truly, I say to you, I am the door of the sheep."

John 10:36 (ESV)
...do you say of Him, whom the Father sanctified and sent into the world, 'You are blaspheming,' because I said, 'I am the Son of God'?

My child,

When you begin to waver, stop and ask is this the truth? Many times opinions are offered as facts, but facts are not always the truth. Look to me and find truth in my word. Remove all other opinions and rest in my truth - this will steady you in mind, soul and spirit.

I Love You ~♥~

James 1:6 (NLT)
But when you ask him, be sure that your faith is in God alone. Do not waver, for a person with divided loyalty is as unsettled as a wave of the sea that is blown and tossed by the wind.

Romans 4:20-25 (MSG)
Abraham didn't focus on his own impotence and say, "It's hopeless. This hundred-year-old body could never father a child." Nor did he survey Sarah's decades of infertility and give up. He didn't tiptoe around God's promise asking cautiously skeptical questions. He plunged into the promise and came up strong, ready for God, sure that God would make good on what he had said. That's why it is said, "Abraham was declared fit before God by trusting God to set him right." But it's not just Abraham; it's also us! The same thing gets said about us when we embrace and believe the One who brought Jesus to life when the conditions were equally hopeless. The sacrificed Jesus made us fit for God, set us right with God.

1 Corinthians 2:4-6 (KJV)
And my speech and my preaching was not with enticing words of man's wisdom, but in demonstration of the Spirit and of power: 5 That your faith should not stand in the wisdom of men, but in the power of God. 6 Howbeit we speak wisdom among them that are perfect: yet not the wisdom of this world, nor of the princes of this world, that come to nought:

2 Timothy 4:5 (AMP)
But as for you, be clear-headed in every situation [stay calm and cool and steady], endure every hardship [without flinching], do the work of an evangelist, fulfill [the duties of] your ministry.

My child,

You first must believe to receive. It is your faith that is pleasing to me. Faith has to be exercised to gain strength. If you want stronger faith, you must believe me for bigger miracles. I stand behind my word - I will deliver!

I Love You ~♥~

Mark 11:24-25 (AMP)

For this reason I am telling you, whatever things you ask for in prayer [in accordance with God's will], believe [with confident trust] that you have received them, and they will be given to you. 25 Whenever you stand praying, if you have anything against anyone, forgive him [drop the issue, let it go], so that your Father who is in heaven will also forgive you your transgressions and wrongdoings [against Him and others].

1 Timothy 4:6-10 (MSG)

You've been raised on the Message of the faith and have followed sound teaching. Now pass on this counsel to the followers of Jesus there, and you'll be a good servant of Jesus. Stay clear of silly stories that get dressed up as religion. Exercise daily in God—no spiritual flabbiness, please! Workouts in the gymnasium are useful, but a disciplined life in God is far more so, making you fit both today and forever. You can count on this. Take it to heart. This is why we've thrown ourselves into this venture so totally. We're banking on the living God, Savior of all men and women, especially believers.

My child,
You are equipped with all that you need to live victoriously. My power is always available to you, but it does require that you stay plugged into the source. Stop proclaiming you are defeated and start praising you are delivered! I Love You ~♥~

Isaiah 41:10-13 (ESV)
fear not, for I am with you; be not dismayed, for I am your God; I will strengthen you, I will help you, I will uphold you with my righteous right hand. Behold, all who are incensed against you shall be put to shame and confounded; those who strive against you shall be as nothing and shall perish. You shall seek those who contend with you, but you shall not find them; those who war against you shall be as nothing at all. For I, the Lord your God, hold your right hand; I who say to you, "Fear not, I am the one who helps you."

1 John 5:4-5 (MSG)
Every God-begotten person conquers the world's ways. The conquering power that brings the world to its knees is our faith. The person who wins out over the world's ways is simply the one who believes Jesus is the Son of God.

2 Corinthians 4:7-9 (EXB)
[But] We have this treasure ·from God, but we are like clay jars that hold the treasure [in clay jars]. This shows that the great [extraordinary; transcendent] power is from God, not from us. We have troubles all around us [or all kinds of troubles/trials], but we are not defeated [crushed]. We do not know what to do [are perplexed/bewildered], but we do not give up the hope of living [despair]. We are persecuted [pursued], but God does not leave us [not abandoned/left behind]. We are hurt [struck down; knocked over] sometimes, but we are not destroyed.

My child,

I am protecting you. Even in times when it appears you are being rejected - rejoice that in me you are protected! I know the plans I have for you - Trust me! Man's rejection is My protection!

I Love You ~♥~

Psalm 27:10 (ESV)
For my father and my mother have forsaken me, but the Lord will take me in.

Philippians 4:19 (AMP)
And my God will liberally supply (fill until full) your every need according to His riches in glory in Christ Jesus.

Psalm 34:17-20 (HCSB)
The righteous cry out, and the Lord hears, and delivers them from all their troubles. 18 The Lord is near the brokenhearted; He saves those crushed in spirit. 19 Many adversities come to the one who is righteous, but the Lord delivers him from them all. 20 He protects all his bones; not one of them is broken.

Psalm 32:8 (KJV)
I will instruct thee and teach thee in the way which thou shalt go: I will guide thee with mine eye.

Jeremiah 29:11-14 (MSG)
This is God's Word on the subject: "As soon as Babylon's seventy years are up and not a day before, I'll show up and take care of you as I promised and bring you back home. I know what I'm doing. I have it all planned out—plans to take care of you, not abandon you, plans to give you the future you hope for. "When you call on me, when you come and pray to me, I'll listen. "When you come looking for me, you'll find me. "Yes, when you get serious about finding me and want it more than anything else, I'll make sure you won't be disappointed." God's Decree.
"I'll turn things around for you. I'll bring you back from all the countries into which I drove you"—God's Decree—"bring you home to the place from which I sent you off into exile. You can count on it.

My Child,

I Love You

My child,

I do not want you sitting around worrying and fretting. You have a life to live and I want you to enjoy your life. You are tormenting yourself trying to have all the answers. Can you be satisfied with knowing that I am the answer? Will you trust me and walk this out believing I am good? If your answer is "yes", then you will be free and much better!

I Love You ~♥~

Philippians 4:6-9 (MSG)
Don't fret or worry. Instead of worrying, pray. Let petitions and praises shape your worries into prayers, letting God know your concerns. Before you know it, a sense of God's wholeness, everything coming together for good, will come and settle you down. It's wonderful what happens when Christ displaces worry at the center of your life. 8-9 Summing it all up, friends, I'd say you'll do best by filling your minds and meditating on things true, noble, reputable, authentic, compelling, gracious—the best, not the worst; the beautiful, not the ugly; things to praise, not things to curse. Put into practice what you learned from me, what you heard and saw and realized. Do that, and God, who makes everything work together, will work you into his most excellent harmonies.

John 14:1 (AMP)
"Do not let your heart be troubled (afraid, cowardly). Believe [confidently] in God and trust in Him, [have faith, hold on to it, rely on it, keep going and] believe also in Me.

My child,

The time has come for you to operate in the authority given to you. No longer will you bow to the idols of this world. Do not believe the false reports given to you. Stand on my truth. Stay close to me, resist the enemy and he will flee. Believe in your heart and speak with your mouth "I am victorious!"

I Love You ~♥~

Ephesians 6:13 (ESV)
Therefore take up the whole armor of God, that you may be able to withstand in the evil day, and having done all, to stand firm.

John 16:13 (AMP)
But when He, the Spirit of Truth, comes, He will guide you into all the truth [full and complete truth]. For He will not speak on His own initiative, but He will speak whatever He hears [from the Father—the message regarding the Son], and He will disclose to you what is to come [in the future].

2 Corinthians 10:4-5 (HCSB)
since the weapons of our warfare are not worldly, but are powerful through God for the demolition of strongholds. We demolish arguments 5 and every high-minded thing that is raised up against the knowledge of God, taking every thought captive to obey Christ.

Jude 24-25 (NLT)
Now all glory to God, who is able to keep you from falling away and will bring you with great joy into his glorious presence without a single fault. 25 All glory to him who alone is God, our Savior through Jesus Christ our Lord. All glory, majesty, power, and authority are his before all time, and in the present, and beyond all time! Amen.

My child,

You must set your mind on eternal things. This world is not your home and you are not to get comfortable here. You are called to be transformed through the renewing of your mind. Do not be conformed to man. You can make a difference by living differently than the world.

I Love You ~♥~

Colossians 3:2 (ESV)
Set your minds on things that are above, not on things that are on earth.

1 Peter 2:11-12 (MSG)
Friends, this world is not your home, so don't make yourselves cozy in it. Don't indulge your ego at the expense of your soul. Live an exemplary life among the natives so that your actions will refute their prejudices. Then they'll be won over to God's side and be there to join in the celebration when he arrives.

Romans 12:2 (NLT)
Don't copy the behavior and customs of this world, but let God transform you into a new person by changing the way you think. Then you will learn to know God's will for you, which is good and pleasing and perfect.

My child,

I hear your prayers for peace. First, you must realize the seeds you're sowing are growing. If you're sowing seeds of discord, you will reap division. I am a God of order. If you want to harvest peace, you must sow peace. Remember, you reap what you sow.

I Love You ~♥~

Proverbs 1:31 (KJV)
Therefore shall they eat of the fruit of their own way, and be filled with their own devices.

Jeremiah 17:10 (NKJV)
I, the Lord, search the heart, I test the mind, Even to give every man according to his ways, According to the fruit of his doings.

Galatians 6:8-9 (HCSB)
...because the one who sows to his flesh will reap corruption from the flesh, but the one who sows to the Spirit will reap eternal life from the Spirit. 9 So we must not get tired of doing good, for we will reap at the proper time if we don't give up.

James 3:17-18 (NIV)
But the wisdom that comes from heaven is first of all pure; then peace-loving, considerate, submissive, full of mercy and good fruit, impartial and sincere. 18 Peacemakers who sow in peace reap a harvest of righteousness.

Hosea 10:12 (ESV)
Sow for yourselves righteousness; reap steadfast love; break up your fallow ground, for it is the time to seek the Lord, that he may come and rain righteousness upon you.

My child,

Vengeance is mine. You do not have to defend yourself or defuse this situation. I am the Lord, your God I will fight for you. Remain in me and allow me full access to your heart. Let me reveal to you any impurities within your heart. That's where it all starts - in the heart. Keep it clean and stay close to me.

I Love You ~♥~

Romans 12:19 (ESV)
Beloved, never avenge yourselves, but leave it to the wrath of God, for it is written, "Vengeance is mine, I will repay, says the Lord."

Psalm 91:14-16 (HCSB)
Because he is lovingly devoted to Me, I will deliver him; I will protect him because he knows My name. 15 When he calls out to Me, I will answer him; I will be with him in trouble. I will rescue him and give him honor. 16 I will satisfy him with a long life and show him My salvation.

Exodus 14:14 (AMP)
The Lord will fight for you while you [only need to] keep silent and remain calm."

Psalm 51:7-15 (MSG)
Soak me in your laundry and I'll come out clean, scrub me and I'll have a snow-white life. Tune me in to foot-tapping songs, set these once-broken bones to dancing. Don't look too close for blemishes, give me a clean bill of health. God, make a fresh start in me, shape a Genesis week from the chaos of my life. Don't throw me out with the trash, or fail to breathe holiness in me. Bring me back from gray exile, put a fresh wind in my sails! Give me a job teaching rebels your ways so the lost can find their way home. Commute my death sentence, God, my salvation God, and I'll sing anthems to your life-giving ways. Unbutton my lips, dear God; I'll let loose with your praise.

My Child,

I Love You

~ ~

Do you want to have it your way or Yahweh?

My child,

Look around at your surroundings. Can you find me in your environment? I have created beautiful things for your enjoyment. Take a few minutes today, slow down and give thanks for the sweet simple things in your life.

I Love You ~♥~

Revelation 4:11 (NIV)
"You are worthy, our Lord and God, to receive glory and honor and power, for you created all things, and by your will they were created and have their being."

Job 12:7-10 (NLT)
"Just ask the animals, and they will teach you. Ask the birds of the sky, and they will tell you. 8 Speak to the earth, and it will instruct you.Let the fish in the sea speak to you. 9 For they all know that my disaster has come from the hand of the Lord. 10 For the life of every living thing is in his hand, and the breath of every human being."

Ecclesiastes 3:9-13 (MSG)
But in the end, does it really make a difference what anyone does? I've had a good look at what God has given us to do—busywork, mostly. True, God made everything beautiful in itself and in its time—but he's left us in the dark, so we can never know what God is up to, whether he's coming or going. I've decided that there's nothing better to do than go ahead and have a good time and get the most we can out of life. That's it—eat, drink, and make the most of your job. It's God's gift.

John 12:28 (NKJV)
"Father, glorify Your name."Then a voice came from heaven, saying, "I have both glorified it and will glorify it again."

My child,

Are you experiencing attacks on all sides of life? I want to remind you the fight is not with flesh and blood. It is indeed a spiritual battle. The darkness is always coming against the light. You have to rise up, use the authority you have been given and speak to every hindering, oppressing and confusing spirit. They are defeated by the blood of JESUS! Victory is yours!

I Love You ~♥~

2 Corinthians 4:8-9 (NLT)
We are pressed on every side by troubles, but we are not crushed. We are perplexed, but not driven to despair. 9 We are hunted down, but never abandoned by God. We get knocked down, but we are not destroyed.

Ephesians 6:12 (AMP)
For our struggle is not against flesh and blood [contending only with physical opponents], but against the rulers, against the powers, against the world forces of this [present] darkness, against the spiritual forces of wickedness in the heavenly (supernatural) places.

Luke 10:19-20 (MSG)
Jesus said, "I know. I saw Satan fall, a bolt of lightning out of the sky. See what I've given you? Safe passage as you walk on snakes and scorpions, and protection from every assault of the Enemy. No one can put a hand on you. All the same, the great triumph is not in your authority over evil, but in God's authority over you and presence with you. Not what you do for God but what God does for you—that's the agenda for rejoicing."

Revelation 12:10-11 (ESV)
And I heard a loud voice in heaven, saying, "Now the salvation and the power and the kingdom of our God and the authority of his Christ have come, for the accuser of our brothers has been thrown down, who accuses them day and night before our God. 11 And they have conquered him by the blood of the Lamb and by the word of their testimony, for they loved not their lives even unto death.

My child,

Freedom is not free. It comes with a great price. You can be free of bondage: Jesus sacrificed his life and gave all he had. Where are you bound? Today, I want you to surrender that to me. The freedom you will receive will set your heart on fire. Release it all and begin your freedom journey.

I Love You ~♥~

Galatians 5:13-14 (ESV)
For you were called to freedom, brothers. Only do not use your freedom as an opportunity for the flesh, but through love serve one another. 14 For the whole law is fulfilled in one word: "You shall love your neighbor as yourself."

Ephesians 3:12 (AMP)
...in whom we have boldness and confident access through faith in Him [that is, our faith gives us sufficient courage to freely and openly approach God through Christ].

1 Peter 2:16 (NLT)
For you are free, yet you are God's slaves, so don't use your freedom as an excuse to do evil.

Psalm 119:41-48 (MSG)
Let your love, God, shape my life with salvation, exactly as you promised; Then I'll be able to stand up to mockery because I trusted your Word. Don't ever deprive me of truth, not ever— your commandments are what I depend on. Oh, I'll guard with my life what you've revealed to me, guard it now, guard it ever; And I'll stride freely through wide open spaces as I look for your truth and your wisdom; Then I'll tell the world what I find, speak out boldly in public, unembarrassed. I cherish your commandments—oh, how I love them!— relishing every fragment of your counsel.

My child,

Do not worry about things beyond your control. It is a waste of your good time. Instead of wasting your time worrying, I want you to worship me. Your life will turn around. I want you to realize that I love you so deeply and I want you to be blessed in this life. I am on your side. Do not fear. Believe and receive - Worship and watch me work.

I Love You ~♥~

Philippians 4:6-7 (MSG)
Don't fret or worry. Instead of worrying, pray. Let petitions and praises shape your worries into prayers, letting God know your concerns. Before you know it, a sense of God's wholeness, everything coming together for good, will come and settle you down. It's wonderful what happens when Christ displaces worry at the center of your life.

Isaiah 43:1-3 (ESV)
But now thus says the Lord, he who created you, O Jacob, he who formed you, O Israel: "Fear not, for I have redeemed you; I have called you by name, you are mine. 2 When you pass through the waters, I will be with you; and through the rivers, they shall not overwhelm you; when you walk through fire you shall not be burned, and the flame shall not consume you. 3 For I am the Lord your God, the Holy One of Israel, your Savior. I give Egypt as your ransom, Cush and Seba in exchange for you.

Romans 8:31 (AMP)
What then shall we say to all these things? If God is for us, who can be [successful] against us?

Psalm 150 (NKJV)
Praise the Lord! Praise God in His sanctuary; Praise Him in His mighty firmament! 2 Praise Him for His mighty acts; Praise Him according to His excellent greatness! 3 Praise Him with the sound of the trumpet; Praise Him with the lute and harp! Praise Him with the timbrel and dance; Praise Him with stringed instruments and flutes! 5 Praise Him with loud cymbals; Praise Him with clashing cymbals! 6 Let everything that has breath praise the Lord. Praise the Lord!

My child,

Get ready for supernatural favor. You have aligned yourself with your divine destiny. Now is the time to step out of the boat and walk on the water. Do not fear for I am near you. We will walk together and miracles will happen. Trust me!

I Love You ~♥~

Proverbs 8:35 (AMP)
"For whoever finds me (Wisdom) finds life And obtains favor and grace from the Lord."

Proverbs 3:4-6 (ESV)
So you will find favor and good success in the sight of God and man.
5 Trust in the Lord with all your heart,and do not lean on your own understanding. 6 In all your ways acknowledge him, and he will make straight your paths.

Zephaniah 3:16-17 (MSG)
Jerusalem will be told: "Don't be afraid. Dear Zion, don't despair.
Your God is present among you, a strong Warrior there to save you.
Happy to have you back, he'll calm you with his love and delight you with his songs."

Matthew 14:27-29 (NKJV)
But immediately Jesus spoke to them, saying, "Be of good cheer! It is I; do not be afraid." 28 And Peter answered Him and said, "Lord, if it is You, command me to come to You on the water." 29 So He said, "Come." And when Peter had come down out of the boat, he walked on the water to go to Jesus.

Psalm 77:14 (NIV)
You are the God who performs miracles; you display your power among the peoples.

My Child,

_____

_____

_____

_____

_____

_____

_____

_____

_____

_____

_____

_____

_____

_____

_____

_____

_____

_____

_____

_____

_____

_____

_____

_____

_____

_____

_____

_____

I Love You

~ ~

A BREAKDOWN comes BEFORE A BREAKTHROUGH

My child,

Be sure you're hearing the right voice. If what you're hearing does not align with my word, then refuse to believe it as truth. You must stay focused in my word, it will lead you on the right path. When in doubt, leave it out!

I Love You ~♥~

John 8:47 (NASB)
"He who is of God hears the words of God; for this reason you do not hear them, because you are not of God."

Jeremiah 33:3 (NASB)
'Call to Me and I will answer you, and I will tell you great and mighty things, which you do not know.'

John 10:27 (ESV)
My sheep hear my voice, and I know them, and they follow me.

Luke 11:28 (HCSB)
He said, "Even more, those who hear the word of God and keep it are blessed!"

Psalm 32:8-9 (MSG)
Let me give you some good advice; I'm looking you in the eye and giving it to you straight: 9 "Don't be ornery like a horse or mule that needs bit and bridle to stay on track."

James 1:22-25 (NLT)
But don't just listen to God's word. You must do what it says. Otherwise, you are only fooling yourselves. 23 For if you listen to the word and don't obey, it is like glancing at your face in a mirror. 24 You see yourself, walk away, and forget what you look like. 25 But if you look carefully into the perfect law that sets you free, and if you do what it says and don't forget what you heard, then God will bless you for doing it.

My child,

Many times I am speaking to you, but you are not listening for me. I do not complicate your life. If you would take time to fellowship with me, the chaos in your life would diminish. Come sit at my feet today. I miss you.

I Love You ~♥~

Job 33:14 (NLT)
For God speaks again and again, though people do not recognize it.

Psalm 27:4 (NIV)
One thing I ask from the Lord, this only do I seek: that I may dwell in the house of the Lord all the days of my life, to gaze on the beauty of the Lord and to seek him in his temple.

1 John 1:3 (ESV)
...that which we have seen and heard we proclaim also to you, so that you too may have fellowship with us; and indeed our fellowship is with the Father and with his Son Jesus Christ.

2 Corinthians 13:11-13 (MSG)
And that's about it, friends. Be cheerful. Keep things in good repair. Keep your spirits up. Think in harmony. Be agreeable. Do all that, and the God of love and peace will be with you for sure. Greet one another with a holy embrace. All the brothers and sisters here say hello.

Luke 10:39-42 (HCSB)
She had a sister named Mary, who also sat at the Lord's feet and was listening to what He said. 40 But Martha was distracted by her many tasks, and she came up and asked, "Lord, don't You care that my sister has left me to serve alone? So tell her to give me a hand." 41 The Lord answered her, "Martha, Martha, you are worried and upset about many things, 42 but one thing is necessary. Mary has made the right choice, and it will not be taken away from her."

My child,

I love you too much to have you remain in the darkness. I know temptations will come, but in those moments you can cry out to me for deliverance. If you will ask me for help and surrender everything, you will overcome!

I Love You ~♥~

Ephesians 5:8 (AMP)
For once you were darkness, but now you are Light in the Lord; walk as children of Light [live as those who are native-born to the Light].

1 Peter 2:9-10 (NKJV)
But you are a chosen generation, a royal priesthood, a holy nation, His own special people, that you may proclaim the praises of Him who called you out of darkness into His marvelous light; 10 who once were not a people but are now the people of God, who had not obtained mercy but now have obtained mercy.

Colossians 1:13-14 (NIV)
For he has rescued us from the dominion of darkness and brought us into the kingdom of the Son he loves, 14 in whom we have redemption, the forgiveness of sins.

1 Corinthians 10:13 (MSG)
No test or temptation that comes your way is beyond the course of what others have had to face. All you need to remember is that God will never let you down; he'll never let you be pushed past your limit; he'll always be there to help you come through it.

1 John 5:4-5 (HCSB)
...because whatever has been born of God conquers the world. This is the victory that has conquered the world: our faith. 5 And who is the one who conquers the world but the one who believes that Jesus is the Son of God?

Revelation 12:11 (NASB)
And they overcame him because of the blood of the Lamb and because of the word of their testimony, and they did not love their life even when faced with death.

My child,

There are circumstances that have occurred in your life that you do not understand. I know you have questioned the purpose for pain or even death. I ask you to step by faith, trusting me to know what is best. Live your life allowing me to have full control. Someday you will understand, but till then just hold my hand.

I Love You ~♥~

Psalm 147:5 (ESV)
Great is our Lord, and abundant in power; his understanding is beyond measure.

Deuteronomy 7:9 (AMP)
Therefore know [without any doubt] and understand that the Lord your God, He is God, the faithful God, who is keeping His covenant and His [steadfast] lovingkindness to a thousand generations with those who love Him and keep His commandments;

Isaiah 45:18 (HCSB)
For this is what the Lord says— God is the Creator of the heavens. He formed the earth and made it. He established it; He did not create it to be empty, but formed it to be inhabited— "I am Yahweh, and there is no other."

Isaiah 55:8-11 (MSG)
"I don't think the way you think. The way you work isn't the way I work." God's Decree. "For as the sky soars high above earth, so the way I work surpasses the way you work, and the way I think is beyond the way you think. Just as rain and snow descend from the skies and don't go back until they've watered the earth, Doing their work of making things grow and blossom, producing seed for farmers and food for the hungry, So will the words that come out of my mouth not come back empty-handed.They'll do the work I sent them to do,they'll complete the assignment I gave them."

Psalm 48:14 (NLT)
For that is what God is like. He is our God forever and ever, and he will guide us until we die.

My child,

You are free to follow me. When you keep your focus upward, you will find freedom from people. Your life isn't about what people think of you; it is what I know about you that truly matters. Let go of the opinions of others and hold to my truth.

I Love You ~♥~

Colossians 3:2 (AMP)
Set your mind and keep focused habitually on the things above [the heavenly things], not on things that are on the earth [which have only temporal value].

John 8:12 (ESV)
Again Jesus spoke to them, saying, "I am the light of the world. Whoever follows me will not walk in darkness, but will have the light of life."

Colossians 2:6-10 (MSG)
My counsel for you is simple and straightforward: Just go ahead with what you've been given. You received Christ Jesus, the Master; now live him. You're deeply rooted in him. You're well-constructed upon him. You know your way around the faith. Now do what you've been taught. School's out; quit studying the subject and start living it! And let your living spill over into thanksgiving. Watch out for people who try to dazzle you with big words and intellectual double-talk. They want to drag you off into endless arguments that never amount to anything. They spread their ideas through the empty traditions of human beings and the empty superstitions of spirit beings. But that's not the way of Christ. Everything of God gets expressed in him, so you can see and hear him clearly. You don't need a telescope, a microscope, or a horoscope to realize the fullness of Christ, and the emptiness of the universe without him. When you come to him, that fullness comes together for you, too. His power extends over everything.

My Child,

I Love You

~~

THERE IS *purpose* IN THE PAIN

My child,

I give rest to the weary. I say come unto to me and I will give you rest. You are in need of spiritual rest and in that you will find physical rest. When you let go of your life, then you will truly live in me.

I Love You ~♥~

Exodus 33:14 (AMP)
And the Lord said, "My presence shall go with you, and I will give you rest [by bringing you and the people into the promised land]."

Psalm 73:26 (ESV)
My flesh and my heart may fail, but God is the strength of my heart and my portion forever.

Psalm 62:1-2 (HCSB)
I am at rest in God alone; my salvation comes from Him. 2 He alone is my rock and my salvation, my stronghold; I will never be shaken.

Hebrews 4:16 (KJV)
Let us therefore come boldly unto the throne of grace, that we may obtain
mercy, and find grace to help in time of need.

Matthew 11:28-30 (MSG)
"Are you tired? Worn out? Burned out on religion? Come to me. Get away with me and you'll recover your life. I'll show you how to take a real rest. Walk with me and work with me—watch how I do it. Learn the unforced rhythms of grace. I won't lay anything heavy or ill-fitting on you. Keep company with me and you'll learn to live freely and lightly."

John 14:27(NLT)
"I am leaving you with a gift—peace of mind and heart. And the peace I give is a gift the world cannot give. So don't be troubled or afraid."

My child,

I am the great physician. I am your God that healeth thee. Will you believe my report over your life? Believe by faith - you are healed!

I Love You ~♥~

Exodus 15:26 (ESV)
...saying, "If you will diligently listen to the voice of the Lord your God, and do that which is right in his eyes, and give ear to his commandments and keep all his statutes, I will put none of the diseases on you that I put on the Egyptians, for I am the Lord, your healer."

Jeremiah 30:17 (AMP)
'For I will restore health to you. And I will heal your wounds,' says the Lord, 'Because they have called you an outcast, saying: "This is Zion; no one seeks her and no one cares for her."'

James 5:13-16 (HCSB)
Is anyone among you suffering? He should pray. Is anyone cheerful? He should sing praises. 14 Is anyone among you sick? He should call for the elders of the church, and they should pray over him after anointing him with olive oil in the name of the Lord. 15 The prayer of faith will save the sick person, and the Lord will restore him to health; if he has committed sins, he will be forgiven. 16 Therefore, confess your sins to one another and pray for one another, so that you may be healed. The urgent request of a righteous person is very powerful in its effect.

Matthew 21:21-22 (NLT)
Then Jesus told them, "I tell you the truth, if you have faith and don't doubt, you can do things like this and much more. You can even say to this mountain, 'May you be lifted up and thrown into the sea,' and it will happen. 22 You can pray for anything, and if you have faith, you will receive it."

My child,

You are always on my mind and heart. I am alert and aware of your situation. Never doubt my abilities. I have full knowledge and all power to work in your life. In order to receive the fullness of my favor, you must rid your heart of offenses. Many of you are offended with me, and that is blocking your blessing. Can you trust me without knowing why certain events took place? Can you believe that I am good and want the best for you? If you say yes, favor will follow!

I Love You ~♥~

Psalm 139:1-6 (MSG)
God, investigate my life; get all the facts firsthand. I'm an open book to you; even from a distance, you know what I'm thinking. You know when I leave and when I get back; I'm never out of your sight. You know everything I'm going to say before I start the first sentence. I look behind me and you're there, then up ahead and you're there, too- your reassuring presence, coming and going. This is too much, too wonderful- I can't take it all in!

Matthew 10:30 (ESV)
But even the hairs of your head are all numbered.

Isaiah 40:26 (HCSB)
Look up and see: who created these? He brings out the starry host by number; He calls all of them by name. Because of His great power and strength, not one of them is missing.

Job 34:21 (KJV)
For his eyes are upon the ways of man, and he seeth all his goings.

2 Chronicles 33:12-13 (HCSB)
When he was in distress, he sought the favor of Yahweh his God and earnestly humbled himself before the God of his ancestors. 13 He prayed to Him, so He heard his petition and granted his request, and brought him back to Jerusalem, to his kingdom. So Manasseh came to know that Yahweh is God.

My child,
Do not allow pride to build walls in your life. You may think this is protection, but it is indeed a self-made prison. You do not have to fear opening your heart to me or others. I am the keeper of the surrendered heart. Lean on me and receive greater love.

I Love You ~♥~

Psalm 10:4 (KJV)
The wicked, through the pride of his countenance, will not seek after God: God is not in all his thoughts.

Proverbs 29:23 (HCSB)
A person's pride will humble him, but a humble spirit will gain honor.

Proverbs 26:12 (AMP)
Do you see a man [who is unteachable and] wise in his own eyes and full of self-conceit? There is more hope for a fool than for him.

Psalm 139:23-24 (MSG)
Investigate my life, O God, find out everything about me; Cross-examine and test me, get a clear picture of what I'm about; See for yourself whether I've done anything wrong— then guide me on the road to eternal life.

Proverbs 23:26 (NIV)
My son, give me your heart and let your eyes delight in my ways,

Ephesians 5:2 (NLT)
Live a life filled with love, following the example of Christ. He loved us and offered himself as a sacrifice for us, a pleasing aroma to God.

My child,

Do not fear others or their evil schemes against your life. Often times you fight the wrong enemy - your battle is not flesh and blood. Your freedom comes when you release people and do not allow them to have power over your life. Set your mind on me.

I Love You ~♥~

Psalm 118:5-9 (ESV)
Out of my distress I called on the Lord; the Lord answered me and set me free. 6 The Lord is on my side; I will not fear. What can man do to me? 7 The Lord is on my side as my helper; I shall look in triumph on those who hate me. 8 It is better to take refuge in the Lord than to trust in man. 9 It is better to take refuge in the Lord than to trust in princes.

Psalm 56:4 (NIV)
In God, whose word I praise— in God I trust and am not afraid. What can mere mortals do to me?

Ephesians 6:12-13 (KJV)
For we wrestle not against flesh and blood, but against principalities, against powers, against the rulers of the darkness of this world, against spiritual wickedness in high places. 13 Wherefore take unto you the whole armour of God, that ye may be able to withstand in the evil day, and having done all, to stand.

Romans 8:31 (NLT)
What shall we say about such wonderful things as these? If God is for us, who can ever be against us?

Colossians 3:2 (NIV)
Set your minds on things above, not on earthly things.

Ephesians 4:22-24 (HCSB)
You took off your former way of life, the old self that is corrupted by deceitful desires; 23 you are being renewed in the spirit of your minds; 24 you put on the new self, the one created according to God's likeness in righteousness and purity of the truth.

My Child,

_____
_____
_____
_____
_____
_____
_____
_____
_____
_____
_____
_____
_____
_____
_____
_____
_____
_____
_____
_____
_____
_____
_____
_____
_____

I Love You

~ ~

believe
for
better

My child,
You do not have to live in cycles of bondage. Taking two steps forward and three steps back. You can be totally free from bowing down to other idols. The blood of JESUS gives you complete access to my freedom. It does require some things of you- humble yourself, submit everything to me and allow my strength to flow through your weak areas. Freedom is here for you!

I Love You ~♥~

2 Peter 2:19 (HCSB)
They promise them freedom, but they themselves are slaves of corruption, since people are enslaved to whatever defeats them.

2 Timothy 2:24-26 (ESV)
And the Lord's servant must not be quarrelsome but kind to everyone, able to teach, patiently enduring evil, 25 correcting his opponents with gentleness. God may perhaps grant them repentance leading to a knowledge of the truth, 26 and they may come to their senses and escape from the snare of the devil, after being captured by him to do his will.

2 Corinthians 10:3-6 (MSG)
The world is unprincipled. It's dog-eat-dog out there! The world doesn't fight fair. But we don't live or fight our battles that way—never have and never will. The tools of our trade aren't for marketing or manipulation, but they are for demolishing that entire massively corrupt culture. We use our powerful God-tools for smashing warped philosophies, tearing down barriers erected against the truth of God, fitting every loose thought and emotion and impulse into the structure of life shaped by Christ. Our tools are ready at hand for clearing the ground of every obstruction and building lives of obedience into maturity.

James 4:7-10 (MSG)
So let God work his will in you. Yell a loud no to the Devil and watch him scamper. Say a quiet yes to God and he'll be there in no time. Quit dabbling in sin. Purify your inner life. Quit playing the field. Hit bottom, and cry your eyes out. The fun and games are over. Get serious, really serious. Get down on your knees before the Master; it's the only way you'll get on your feet.

My child,

There is power in your words. Life and death have the ability to come from your tongue through your words. Take time to examine your heart before you speak your words. Let life come forth out of your mouth. You receive what you speak. Let your words be kind, loving and encouraging. Your life will follow your words.

I Love You ~♥~

Proverbs 18:21 (AMP)
Death and life are in the power of the tongue, And those who love it and indulge it will eat its fruit and bear the consequences of their words.

Proverbs 29:20 (ESV)
Do you see a man who is hasty in his words? There is more hope for a fool than for him.

Luke 6:45 (NIV)
A good man brings good things out of the good stored up in his heart, and an evil man brings evil things out of the evil stored up in his heart. For the mouth speaks what the heart is full of.

Psalm 19:14 (KJV)
Let the words of my mouth, and the meditation of my heart, be acceptable in thy sight, O Lord, my strength, and my redeemer.

Ephesians 4:29 (MSG)
Watch the way you talk. Let nothing foul or dirty come out of your mouth. Say only what helps, each word a gift.

Proverbs 12:18 (HCSB)
There is one who speaks rashly, like a piercing sword; but the tongue of the wise brings healing.

1 Thessalonians 5:11 (NLT)
So encourage each other and build each other up, just as you are already doing.

My child,

Are you putting me first in your life? Am I the first thing you think about when you wake up in the morning? Do you consider me first before making decisions? If you are going to experience the abundant life that I've promised you, I must be first - above everything and everyone. Seek me first and you will never have to worry about being last.

I Love You ~♥~

1 Kings 22:5 (NLT)
Then Jehoshaphat added, "But first let's find out what the Lord says."

Proverbs 8:17 (KJV)
I love them that love me; and those that seek me early shall find me.

Mark 1:35 (AMP)
Early in the morning, while it was still dark, Jesus got up, left [the house], and went out to a secluded place, and was praying there.

Psalm 5:3 (NIV)
In the morning, Lord, you hear my voice; in the morning I lay my requests before you and wait expectantly.

Matthew 6:33 (ESV)
But seek first the kingdom of God and his righteousness, and all these things will be added to you.

Deuteronomy 4:29-31 (MSG)
But even there, if you seek God, your God, you'll be able to find him if you're serious, looking for him with your whole heart and soul. When troubles come and all these awful things happen to you, in future days you will come back to God, your God, and listen obediently to what he says. God, your God, is above all a compassionate God. In the end he will not abandon you, he won't bring you to ruin, he won't forget the covenant with your ancestors which he swore to them.

Hebrews 11:6 (NASB)
And without faith it is impossible to please Him, for he who comes to God must believe that He is and that He is a rewarder of those who seek Him.

My child,

Where is your true heart for me? You may say, "I'm doing all of this for you, Lord." All the while, I do not know your heart. What good is the work in my name, if I am not a part of the game? Examine your heart and see where I fit in or if I am even there at all. Don't get distracted working for me that you forget to include me.

I LoveYou ~♥~

Nehemiah 1:9 (HCSB)
"But if you return to Me and carefully observe My commands, even though your exiles were banished to the ends of the earth, I will gather them from there and bring them to the place where I chose to have My name dwell."

Matthew 7:21-23 (MSG)
"Knowing the correct password—saying 'Master, Master,' for instance—isn't going to get you anywhere with me. What is required is serious obedience—doing what my Father wills. I can see it now—at the Final Judgment thousands strutting up to me and saying, 'Master, we preached the Message, we bashed the demons, our God-sponsored projects had everyone talking.' And do you know what I am going to say? 'You missed the boat. All you did was use me to make yourselves important. You don't impress me one bit. You're out of here.'

James 4:8 (NLT)
Come close to God, and God will come close to you. Wash your hands, you sinners; purify your hearts, for your loyalty is divided between God and the world.

Jeremiah 24:7 (KJV)
And I will give them an heart to know me, that I am the Lord: and they shall be my people, and I will be their God: for they shall return unto me with their whole heart.

My child,

You are not forgotten by me, I am the GOD who sees. I am closer than you could ever imagine. If you will choose to look through your spiritual eyes, you will see me. When you see me, then all the worldly distractions will grow dim. Look upward to me; not outward to man.

I Love You ~♥~

Isaiah 49:15 (NLT)
"Never! Can a mother forget her nursing child? Can she feel no love for the child she has borne? But even if that were possible, I would not forget you."

Genesis 16:13 (NIV)
She gave this name to the LORD who spoke to her: "You are the God who sees me," for she said, "I have now seen the One who sees me."

Proverbs 15:3 (AMP)
The eyes of the Lord are in every place, Watching the evil and the good [in all their endeavors].

Psalm 32:8 (HCSB)
I will instruct you and show you the way to go; with My eye on you, I will give counsel.

2 Corinthians 4:18 (KJV)
While we look not at the things which are seen, but at the things which are not seen: for the things which are seen are temporal; but the things which are not seen are eternal.

My Child,

_____
_____
_____
_____
_____
_____
_____
_____
_____
_____
_____
_____
_____
_____
_____
_____
_____
_____
_____
_____
_____
_____
_____
_____
_____
_____
_____

I Love You

~ ~

too BLESSED to be STRESSED

My child,

When you fully trust me, you will experience peace and contentment. Having Godly contentment regardless of your circumstances removes all strife from your life. Today, will you resolve in your heart to be content? You will find unwavering peace through me.

I Love You ~♥~

Timothy 6:6-7 (ESV)
But godliness with contentment is great gain, 7 for we brought nothing into the world, and we cannot take anything out of the world.

1 Corinthians 7:20-24 (HCSB)
Each person should remain in the life situation in which he was called. 21 Were you called while a slave? It should not be a concern to you. But if you can become free, by all means take the opportunity. 22 For he who is called by the Lord as a slave is the Lord's freedman. Likewise he who is called as a free man is Christ's slave. 23 You were bought at a price; do not become slaves of men. 24 Brothers, each person should remain with God in whatever situation he was called.

1 Timothy 6:8 (KJV)
And having food and raiment let us be therewith content.

Philippians 4:10-14 (MSG)
I'm glad in God, far happier than you would ever guess—happy that you're again showing such strong concern for me. Not that you ever quit praying and thinking about me. You just had no chance to show it. Actually, I don't have a sense of needing anything personally. I've learned by now to be quite content whatever my circumstances. I'm just as happy with little as with much, with much as with little. I've found the recipe for being happy whether full or hungry, hands full or hands empty. Whatever I have, wherever I am, I can make it through anything in the One who makes me who I am. I don't mean that your help didn't mean a lot to me—it did. It was a beautiful thing that you came alongside me in my troubles.

James 3:17 (NASB)
But the wisdom from above is first pure, then peaceable, gentle, reasonable, full of mercy and good fruits, unwavering, without hypocrisy.

My child,

You have come too far to turn back now. I know life can be tough and you have questions of why certain thing had to happen in your life. Be encouraged today - what you're going through; will not overcome you! Together, you and I are stronger. Call out to me and I will answer. Daily decide to move closer to me. I Love You ~♥~

Philippians 3:14-16 (HCSB)
I pursue as my goal the prize promised by God's heavenly call in Christ Jesus. 15 Therefore, all who are mature should think this way. And if you think differently about anything, God will reveal this also to you. 16 In any case, we should live up to whatever truth we have attained.

Joshua 1:7-9 (ESV)
Only be strong and very courageous, being careful to do according to all the law that Moses my servant commanded you. Do not turn from it to the right hand or to the left, that you may have good success wherever you go. 8 This Book of the Law shall not depart from your mouth, but you shall meditate on it day and night, so that you may be careful to do according to all that is written in it. For then you will make your way prosperous, and then you will have good success. 9 Have I not commanded you? Be strong and courageous. Do not be frightened, and do not be dismayed, for the Lord your God is with you wherever you go."

1 Peter 2:19-20 (KJV)
For this is thankworthy, if a man for conscience toward God endure grief, suffering wrongfully. 20 For what glory is it, if, when ye be buffeted for your faults, ye shall take it patiently? but if, when ye do well, and suffer for it, ye take it patiently, this is acceptable with God.

1 Thessalonians 3:3-5 (MSG)
Not that the troubles should come as any surprise to you. You've always known that we're in for this kind of thing. It's part of our calling. When we were with you, we made it quite clear that there was trouble ahead. And now that it's happened, you know what it's like. That's why I couldn't quit worrying; I had to know for myself how you were doing in the faith. I didn't want the Tempter getting to you and tearing down everything we had built up together.

My child,

Time and time again you have tried to prove your love for me. I want you to know once and for all that I see your heart. Your outer works do not impress me, I know your heart motives behind the actions. Today, examine your heart. It's not always easy to look inside your soul, but it is necessary.

I Love You ~♥~

Jeremiah 17:9-10 (MSG)
"The heart is hopelessly dark and deceitful, a puzzle that no one can figure out. But I, God, search the heart and examine the mind. I get to the heart of the human. I get to the root of things. I treat them as they really are, not as they pretend to be."

Proverbs 16:2 (NIV)
All a person's ways seem pure to them, but motives are weighed by the Lord.

Matthew 6:1 (ESV)
"Beware of practicing your righteousness before other people in order to be seen by them, for then you will have no reward from your Father who is in heaven."

Galatians 4:9-11 (NLT)
So now that you know God (or should I say, now that God knows you), why do you want to go back again and become slaves once more to the weak and useless spiritual principles of this world? 10 You are trying to earn favor with God by observing certain days or months or seasons or years. 11 I fear for you. Perhaps all my hard work with you was for nothing.

2 Corinthians 13:5 (AMP)
Test and evaluate yourselves to see whether you are in the faith and living your lives as [committed] believers. Examine yourselves [not me]! Or do you not recognize this about yourselves [by an ongoing experience] that Jesus Christ is in you—unless indeed you fail the test and are rejected as counterfeit?

My child,
I am continually moving in your midst. My Spirit is ever flowing through you. When you walk by my Spirit, you are empowered to do that which appears impossible. Stay in alignment with your assignment. A wonder-filled future is ahead of you.

I Love You ~♥~

2 Corinthians 12:9 (AMP)
...but He has said to me, "My grace is sufficient for you [My lovingkindness and My mercy are more than enough—always available—regardless of the situation]; for [My] power is being perfected [and is completed and shows itself most effectively] in [your] weakness." Therefore, I will all the more gladly boast in my weaknesses, so that the power of Christ [may completely enfold me and] may dwell in me.

2 Corinthians 4:16-18 (ESV)
So we do not lose heart. Though our outer self is wasting away, our inner self is being renewed day by day. 17 For this light momentary affliction is preparing for us an eternal weight of glory beyond all comparison, 18 as we look not to the things that are seen but to the things that are unseen. For the things that are seen are transient, but the things that are unseen are eternal.

2 Peter 1:3-7 (KJV)
According as his divine power hath given unto us all things that pertain unto life and godliness, through the knowledge of him that hath called us to glory and virtue: Whereby are given unto us exceeding great and precious promises: that by these ye might be partakers of the divine nature, having escaped the corruption that is in the world through lust. And beside this, giving all diligence, add to your faith virtue; and to virtue knowledge; And to knowledge temperance; and to temperance patience; and to patience godliness; And to godliness brotherly kindness; and to brotherly kindness charity.

My child,

I am the God of restoration. I can bring what's dead back to life. Is your marriage needing life? How about family relationships? Are your emotions lacking life? There are powerful forces at work to rob, steal and destroy you. Rise up, plead the blood of Jesus over your marriage, family and yourself. There is life in the blood of the Lamb!
I Love You

Psalm 51:12 (AMP)
Restore to me the joy of Your salvation And sustain me with a willing spirit.

Ezekiel 16:8 (ESV)
"When I passed by you again and saw you, behold, you were at the age for love, and I spread the corner of my garment over you and covered your nakedness; I made my vow to you and entered into a covenant with you, declares the Lord God, and you became mine.

Hebrews 13:4 (HCSB)
Marriage must be respected by all, and the marriage bed kept undefiled, because God will judge immoral people and adulterers.

Matthew 5:24 (KJV)
Leave there thy gift before the altar, and go thy way; first be reconciled to thy brother, and then come and offer thy gift.

Hebrews 9:22 (NIV)
In fact, the law requires that nearly everything be cleansed with blood, and without the shedding of blood there is no forgiveness.

Isaiah 1:18-20 (MSG)
"Come. Sit down. Let's argue this out." This is God's Message:
"If your sins are blood-red, they'll be snow-white. If they're red like crimson, they'll be like wool. If you'll willingly obey, you'll feast like kings. But if you're willful and stubborn, you'll die like dogs." That's right. God says so.

My Child,

I Love You

YOU'RE NOT built FOR guilt

My child,

When true contentment comes, your words will be few. It's only when you feel unnoticed by others that a need arises to be heard. Well, let me assure you this day - I hear you. I am aware, alert and I am listening to you. Be encouraged and content, knowing I am near. You can remain confident and silent knowing I am with you.

I Love You ~♥~

1 John 4:6 (HCSB)
We are from God. Anyone who knows God listens to us; anyone who is not from God does not listen to us. From this we know the Spirit of truth and the spirit of deception.

Philippians 4:10-14 (MSG)
I'm glad in God, far happier than you would ever guess—happy that you're again showing such strong concern for me. Not that you ever quit praying and thinking about me. You just had no chance to show it. Actually, I don't have a sense of needing anything personally. I've learned by now to be quite content whatever my circumstances. I'm just as happy with little as with much, with much as with little. I've found the recipe for being happy whether full or hungry, hands full or hands empty. Whatever I have, wherever I am, I can make it through anything in the One who makes me who I am. I don't mean that your help didn't mean a lot to me—it did. It was a beautiful thing that you came alongside me in my troubles.

Psalm 121:7-8 (MSG)
God guards you from every evil, he guards your very life. He guards you when you leave and when you return, he guards you now, he guards you always.

Ephesians 3:12 (NIV)
In him and through faith in him we may approach God with freedom and
confidence.

My child,

Slow down - don't get in a hurry. The world you live in is fast paced and full of pressure. Why do you have impatience waiting on me? I am not on the watch clock of the world. I have my own timing and I am teaching you that my timing is perfect. Your time is in my hands. If you will surrender your time, trust me as you wait, you will find deeper endurance and faith in me.

I Love You. ~♥~

Psalm 31:15 (AMP)
My times are in Your hands; Rescue me from the hand of my enemies and from those who pursue and persecute me.

Psalm 46:10-11 (ESV)
"Be still, and know that I am God. I will be exalted among the nations,I will be exalted in the earth!" 11 The Lord of hosts is with us; the God of Jacob is our fortress.

Luke 10:38-42 (HCSB)
While they were traveling, He entered a village, and a woman named Martha welcomed Him into her home. 39 She had a sister named Mary, who also sat at the Lord's feet and was listening to what He said. 40 But Martha was distracted by her many tasks, and she came up and asked, "Lord, don't You care that my sister has left me to serve alone? So tell her to give me a hand." 41 The Lord answered her, "Martha, Martha, you are worried and upset about many things, 42 but one thing is necessary. Mary has made the right choice, and it will not be taken away from her."

Psalm 62:5-6 (NIV)
Yes, my soul, find rest in God; my hope comes from him. 6 Truly he is my rock and my salvation; he is my fortress, I will not be shaken.

James 5:7-8 (NLT)
Dear brothers and sisters, be patient as you wait for the Lord's return. Consider the farmers who patiently wait for the rains in the fall and in the spring. They eagerly look for the valuable harvest to ripen. 8 You, too, must be patient. Take courage, for the coming of the Lord is near.

My child,
Everything you are worrying about is out of your control. I want you to take the wasted time used on worry and give it to me. I have many blessings to send you, but they are being blocked by your worry. Do you believe what you are thinking and speaking or do you believe my word? Trust me completely and you will find me. Worship me, not the worthless idol of worry.

I Love You ~♥~

Psalm 39:4-5 (ESV)
"O Lord, make me know my end and what is the measure of my days; let me know how fleeting I am! 5 Behold, you have made my days a few handbreadths, and my lifetime is as nothing before you.
Surely all mankind stands as a mere breath! Selah

Proverbs 12:25 (AMP)
Anxiety in a man's heart weighs it down,But a good (encouraging) word makes it glad.

Matthew 12:37 (NKJV)
For by your words you will be justified, and by your words you will be condemned."

Proverbs 18:21 (MSG)
Words kill, words give life; they're either poison or fruit—you choose.

Jeremiah 2:8 (NLT)
The priests did not ask, 'Where is the LORD?' Those who taught my word ignored me, the rulers turned against me, and the prophets spoke in the name of Baal, wasting their time on worthless idols.

My child,

I want to lavish my love on you. Take a few minutes today, open your heart up to me and receive my love. I will mend your brokenness and build you stronger. You must trust me with this process. My love will never fail you. Let me love you the way you deserve to be loved.

I Love You ~♥~

1 John 3:1 (NIV)
See what great love the Father has lavished on us, that we should be called children of God! And that is what we are! The reason the world does not know us is that it did not know him.

Deuteronomy 7:9-10 (MSG)
God wasn't attracted to you and didn't choose you because you were big and important—the fact is, there was almost nothing to you. He did it out of sheer love, keeping the promise he made to your ancestors. God stepped in and mightily bought you back out of that world of slavery, freed you from the iron grip of Pharaoh king of Egypt. Know this: God, your God, is God indeed, a God you can depend upon. He keeps his covenant of loyal love with those who love him and observe his commandments for a thousand generations. But he also pays back those who hate him, pays them the wages of death; he isn't slow to pay them off—those who hate him, he pays right on time.

Colossians 2:6-7 (HCSB)
Therefore, as you have received Christ Jesus the Lord, walk in Him, 7 rooted and built up in Him and established in the faith, just as you were taught, overflowing with gratitude.

1 Corinthians 13:8-10 (MSG)
Love never dies. Inspired speech will be over some day; praying in tongues will end; understanding will reach its limit. We know only a portion of the truth, and what we say about God is always incomplete. But when the Complete arrives, our incompletes will be canceled.

My child,

I know you are dealing with frustrations. But, I want you to realize what you are experiencing is not coming from external pressures. Stop focusing on that which you have no control over and look within. Your frustration comes from an internal conflict with your heart. You are disappointed within yourself. Give yourself some grace and remove your critical eye. When you mess up, fess up and move on. You will find peace on the inside, and it will radiate on the outside. You are forgiven, it's time to walk in freedom!

I Love You ~♥~

Romans 7:14-20 (MSG)
I can anticipate the response that is coming: "I know that all God's commands are spiritual, but I'm not. Isn't this also your experience?" Yes. I'm full of myself—after all, I've spent a long time in sin's prison. What I don't understand about myself is that I decide one way, but then I act another, doing things I absolutely despise. So if I can't be trusted to figure out what is best for myself and then do it, it becomes obvious that God's command is necessary. 17-20 But I need something more! For if I know the law but still can't keep it, and if the power of sin within me keeps sabotaging my best intentions, I obviously need help! I realize that I don't have what it takes. I can will it, but I can't do it. I decide to do good, but I don't really do it; I decide not to do bad, but then I do it anyway. My decisions, such as they are, don't result in actions. Something has gone wrong deep within me and gets the better of me every time.

Philippians 1:6 (HCSB)
I am sure of this, that He who started a good work in you will carry it on to completion until the day of Christ Jesus.

Philippians 4:8 (ESV)
Finally, brothers, whatever is true, whatever is honorable, whatever is just, whatever is pure, whatever is lovely, whatever is commendable, if there is any excellence, if there is anything worthy of praise, think about these things.

My Child,

_____
_____
_____
_____
_____
_____
_____
_____
_____
_____
_____
_____
_____
_____
_____
_____
_____
_____
_____
_____
_____
_____
_____
_____
_____
_____
_____
_____
_____
_____
_____

I Love You

~ ~

My child,

When you live your life with me as your first priority, you will not get stuck. It's only the times you run off the path that I've placed before you that you get stuck. Stop, refocus yourself and ask me to show you the way. You will get moving again. You are not stuck, you're just experiencing a slowdown. Keep moving with me.

I Love You ~♥~

Psalm 25:4-53 (AMP)
Let me know Your ways, O Lord; Teach me Your paths. 5 Guide me in Your truth and teach me, For You are the God of my salvation; For You [and only You] I wait [expectantly] all the day long.

Psalm 61:1-3 (ESV)
Hear my cry, O God, listen to my prayer; 2 from the end of the earth I call to you when my heart is faint. Lead me to the rock that is higher than I, 3 for you have been my refuge, a strong tower against the enemy.

Psalm 143:8 (NLT)
Let me hear of your unfailing love each morning, for I am trusting you. Show me where to walk, for I give myself to you.

Acts 17:28-29 (MSG)
"The God who made the world and everything in it, this Master of sky and land, doesn't live in custom-made shrines or need the human race to run errands for him, as if he couldn't take care of himself. He makes the creatures; the creatures don't make him. Starting from scratch, he made the entire human race and made the earth hospitable, with plenty of time and space for living so we could seek after God, and not just grope around in the dark but actually find him. He doesn't play hide-and-seek with us. He's not remote; he's near. We live and move in him, can't get away from him! One of your poets said it well: 'We're the God-created.' Well, if we are the God-created, it doesn't make a lot of sense to think we could hire a sculptor to chisel a god out of stone for us, does it?

My child,

From time to time you may be misjudged or misunderstood, but I know who you are and what you're about. Do not fear the words of man over your life. Believe my words and stand on my truth. Even if rejection seems to be all around you - I accept you for who you are and how I created you. You are set apart for my kingdom- just know you will not fit in this world.

I Love You ~♥~

Luke 5:20-25 (NLT)
Seeing their faith, Jesus said to the man, "Young man, your sins are forgiven." 21 But the Pharisees and teachers of religious law said to themselves, "Who does he think he is? That's blasphemy! Only God can forgive sins!" 22 Jesus knew what they were thinking, so he asked them, "Why do you question this in your hearts? 23 Is it easier to say 'Your sins are forgiven,' or 'Stand up and walk'? 24 So I will prove to you that the Son of Man has the authority on earth to forgive sins." Then Jesus turned to the paralyzed man and said, "Stand up, pick up your mat, and go home!" 25 And immediately, as everyone watched, the man jumped up, picked up his mat, and went home praising God.

John 10:14-18 (MSG)
"I am the Good Shepherd. I know my own sheep and my own sheep know me. In the same way, the Father knows me and I know the Father. I put the sheep before myself, sacrificing myself if necessary. You need to know that I have other sheep in addition to those in this pen. I need to gather and bring them, too. They'll also recognize my voice. Then it will be one flock, one Shepherd. This is why the Father loves me: because I freely lay down my life. And so I am free to take it up again. No one takes it from me. I lay it down of my own free will. I have the right to lay it down; I also have the right to take it up again. I received this authority personally from my Father."

My child,

Do not place your destiny in the hands of others. You can have peace, joy, happiness and love regardless of others. When you allow them to interfere with me, you are choosing to place your destiny in their hands. I hold your future and all that's in it. Do not bow to the spirit of intimidation; stand firm on my true unwavering foundation.

I Love You ~♥~

Jeremiah 17:7-8 (AMP)
"Blessed [with spiritual security] is the man who believes and trusts in and relies on the Lord And whose hope and confident expectation is the Lord. 8 "For he will be [nourished] like a tree planted by the waters, That spreads out its roots by the river; And will not fear the heat when it comes; But its leaves will be green and moist. And it will not be anxious and concerned in a year of drought Nor stop bearing fruit.

Psalm 143:8 (ESV)
Let me hear in the morning of your steadfast love, for in you I trust.
Make me know the way I should go, for to you I lift up my soul.

Psalm 73:25-26 (HCSB)
Who do I have in heaven but You? And I desire nothing on earth but You. 26 My flesh and my heart may fail, but God is the strength of my heart, my portion forever.

Proverbs 29:25-27 (MSG)
The fear of human opinion disables; trusting in God protects you from that. 26 Everyone tries to get help from the leader, but only God will give us justice. 27 Good people can't stand the sight of deliberate evil; the wicked can't stand the sight of well-chosen goodness.

Hebrews 13:6 (NLT)
So we can say with confidence,"The Lord is my helper, so I will have no fear. What can mere people do to me?"

My child,

Living your life through my Spirit is not complicated. When confusion and chaos come, that can be an indication you are walking by your own strength and not through my Spirit. Take a step back and ask me for clarity. I will simplify your life and give you a clear perspective.

I Love You ~♥~

Ezekiel 36:27 (KJV)
And I will put my spirit within you, and cause you to walk in my statutes, and ye shall keep my judgments, and do them.

2 Timothy 1:14 (NLT)
Through the power of the Holy Spirit who lives within us, carefully guard the precious truth that has been entrusted to you.

Romans 8:9-11 (NIV)
You, however, are not in the realm of the flesh but are in the realm of the Spirit, if indeed the Spirit of God lives in you. And if anyone does not have the Spirit of Christ, they do not belong to Christ. 10 But if Christ is in you, then even though your body is subject to death because of sin, the Spirit gives life because of righteousness. 11 And if the Spirit of him who raised Jesus from the dead is living in you, he who raised Christ from the dead will also give life to your mortal bodies because of his Spirit who lives in you.

1 John 2:26-27 (MSG)
I've written to warn you about those who are trying to deceive you. But they're no match for what is embedded deeply within you—Christ's anointing, no less! You don't need any of their so-called teaching. Christ's anointing teaches you the truth on everything you need to know about yourself and him, uncontaminated by a single lie. Live deeply in what you were taught.

My child,

In my name you have victory. No other name that you proclaim can accomplish an eternal work of your soul. Call out my name today. I love to hear you say my name. When you call upon my name, I will answer and deliver you.

I Love You ~♥~

Philippians 2:9-11 (AMP)
For this reason also [because He obeyed and so completely humbled Himself], God has highly exalted Him and bestowed on Him the name which is above every name, 10 so that at the name of Jesus every knee shall bow [in submission], of those who are in heaven and on earth and under the earth, 11 and that every tongue will confess and openly acknowledge that Jesus Christ is Lord (sovereign God), to the glory of God the Father.

Psalm 86:5 (ESV)
For you, O Lord, are good and forgiving ,abounding in steadfast love to all who call upon you.

Psalm 50:15 (KJV)
And call upon me in the day of trouble: I will deliver thee, and thou shalt glorify me.

Lamentations 3:55-58 (NIV)
I called on your name, Lord, from the depths of the pit. 56 You heard my plea: "Do not close your ears to my cry for relief." 57 You came near when I called you, and you said, "Do not fear." 58 You, Lord, took up my case; you redeemed my life.

Psalm 17:6-9 (NLT)
I am praying to you because I know you will answer, O God. Bend down and listen as I pray. 7 Show me your unfailing love in wonderful ways. By your mighty power you rescue those who seek refuge from their enemies. 8 Guard me as you would guard your own eyes. Hide me in the shadow of your wings. 9 Protect me from wicked people who attack me, from murderous enemies who surround me.

My Child,

I Love You

~ ~

meekness IS NOT weakness

My child,

Do you not understand that in this world you own nothing? As my child, everything and everyone belongs to me. When you come to the place of letting go of all that you are holding on to, you will find true freedom in me. Surrender your family, finances and future; by doing this you will find deeper faith to follow me. I have greater blessings that go beyond this world.

I Love You ~♥~

1 Timothy 6:7 (KJV)
For we brought nothing into this world, and it is certain we can carry nothing out.

2 Corinthians 6:9-10 (AMP)
...as unknown [to the world], yet well-known [by God and His people]; as dying, yet we live; as punished, yet not killed; 10 as sorrowful, yet always rejoicing; as poor, yet bestowing riches on many; as having nothing, yet possessing all things.

Psalm 24:1 (NLT)
The earth is the Lord's, and everything in it. The world and all its people belong to him.

Hebrews 2:10 (CEV)
Everything belongs to God, and all things were created by his power. So God did the right thing when he made Jesus perfect by suffering, as Jesus led many of God's children to be saved and to share in his glory.

Psalm 34:17-19 (HCSB)
The righteous cry out, and the Lord hears, and delivers them from all their troubles. 18 The Lord is near the brokenhearted; He saves those crushed in spirit. 19 Many adversities come to the one who is righteous, but the Lord delivers him from them all.

My child,

Set a guard over your mind. Do not allow the enemy to plant false thoughts in your mind. What you think will determine where you go. Look up and allow me to transform your thoughts by removing all the rotten, wrong stinking thinking. I've created and placed beauty all around you - take delight and dwell on these things.

I Love you ~♥~

Philippians 4:6-8 (NIV)
Do not be anxious about anything, but in every situation, by prayer and petition, with thanksgiving, present your requests to God. 7 And the peace of God, which transcends all understanding, will guard your hearts and your minds in Christ Jesus. 8 Finally, brothers and sisters, whatever is true, whatever is noble, whatever is right, whatever is pure, whatever is lovely, whatever is admirable—if anything is excellent or praiseworthy—think about such things.

2 Corinthians 10:3-5 (HCSB)
For though we live in the body, do not wage war in an unspiritual way, 4 since the weapons of our warfare are not worldly, but are powerful through God for the demolition of strongholds. We demolish arguments 5 and every high-minded thing that is raised up against the knowledge of God, taking every thought captive to obey Christ.

Proverbs 4:25-27 (NIV)
Let your eyes look straight ahead; fix your gaze directly before you.
26 Give careful thought to the paths for your feet and be steadfast in all your ways. 27 Do not turn to the right or the left; keep your foot from evil.

2 Corinthians 10:5 (KJV)
Casting down imaginations, and every high thing that exalteth itself against the knowledge of God, and bringing into captivity every thought to the obedience of Christ;

My child,

True independence comes from being dependent on me. I am always here for you. You are never without my help through this life you are living. Lean on me, trust me and allow me to come to your rescue. I do not view you as being weak, but wise when you fully rely on me. Resist the whispers of the enemy that condemns you for depending on me.

I Love You ~♥~

Psalm 33:20-22 (MSG)
We're depending on God; he's everything we need. What's more, our hearts brim with joy since we've taken for our own his holy name. Love us, God, with all you've got— that's what we're depending on.

Psalm 44:3 (NLT)
They did not conquer the land with their swords; it was not their own strong arm that gave them victory. It was your right hand and strong arm and the blinding light from your face that helped them, for you loved them.

1 Chronicles 29:14 (HCSB)
But who am I, and who are my people, that we should be able to give as generously as this? For everything comes from You, and we have given You only what comes from Your own hand.

Psalm 73:26 (ESV)
My flesh and my heart may fail, but God is the strength of my heart and my portion forever.

1 Peter 5:8 (KJV)
Be sober, be vigilant; because your adversary the devil, as a roaring lion,
walketh about, seeking whom he may devour:

My child,

Today I want you to take an assessment of how well you are shining my light in this sin-sick dark world. Use my word as the plumb line; do not measure yourself against another. You are called out of darkness; do not engage in worldly pleasures. This only hinders my radiant light. Do not hide my light to be accepted by the world. You will lead them to me by allowing my light to shine through you.

I Love You ~♥~

Romans 13:11-14 (AMP)
Do this, knowing that this is a critical time. It is already the hour for you to awaken from your sleep [of spiritual complacency]; for our salvation is nearer to us now than when we first believed [in Christ]. 12 The night [this present evil age] is almost gone and the day [of Christ's return] is almost here. So let us fling away the works of darkness and put on the [full] armor of light. 13 Let us conduct ourselves properly and honorably as in the [light of] day, not in carousing and drunkenness, not in sexual promiscuity and irresponsibility, not in quarreling and jealousy. 14 But clothe yourselves with the Lord Jesus Christ, and make no provision for [nor even think about gratifying] the flesh in regard to its improper desires.

Colossians 1:9-14 (MSG)
Be assured that from the first day we heard of you, we haven't stopped praying for you, asking God to give you wise minds and spirits attuned to his will, and so acquire a thorough understanding of the ways in which God works. We pray that you'll live well for the Master, making him proud of you as you work hard in his orchard. As you learn more and more how God works, you will learn how to do your work. We pray that you'll have the strength to stick it out over the long haul—not the grim strength of gritting your teeth but the glory-strength God gives. It is strength that endures the unendurable and spills over into joy, thanking the Father who makes us strong enough to take part in everything bright and beautiful that he has for us. 13-14 God rescued us from dead-end alleys and dark dungeons. He's set us up in the kingdom of the Son he loves so much, the Son who got us out of the pit we were in, got rid of the sins we were doomed to keep repeating.

My child,

Your days on earth are numbered. What are you doing with your time? Don't be wasteful, use your time wisely. Make the most of what you've been given. All your days are filled with purpose. It's your mission to discover my purpose during the day. If you will place me in the center of your day, you will find the balance you need. I Love You ~♥~

Job 14:5 (NKJV)
Since his days are determined, The number of his months is with You; You have appointed his limits, so that he cannot pass.

Psalm 39: 4-13 (NLT)
" LORD, remind me how brief my time on earth will be. Remind me that my days are numbered— how fleeting my life is. 5 You have made my life no longer than the width of my hand. My entire lifetime is just a moment to you; at best, each of us is but a breath." Interlude 6 We are merely moving shadows, and all our busy rushing ends in nothing. We heap up wealth, not knowing who will spend it. 7 And so, Lord, where do I put my hope? My only hope is in you. 8 Rescue me from my rebellion. Do not let fools mock me. 9 I am silent before you; I won't say a word, for my punishment is from you. 10 But please stop striking me! I am exhausted by the blows from your hand. 11 When you discipline us for our sins, you consume like a moth what is precious to us. Each of us is but a breath. Interlude 12 Hear my prayer, O LORD ! Listen to my cries for help! Don't ignore my tears. For I am your guest— a traveler passing through, as my ancestors were before me. 13 Leave me alone so I can smile again before I am gone and exist no more.

Proverbs 20:24 (NKJV)
A man's steps are of the Lord; How then can a man understand his own way?
2 Timothy 1:9 (AMP)
for He delivered us and saved us and called us with a holy calling [a calling that leads to a consecrated life—a life set apart—a life of purpose], not because of our works [or because of any personal merit—we could do nothing to earn this], but because of His own purpose and grace [His amazing, undeserved favor] which was granted to us in Christ Jesus before the world began [eternal ages ago].

My Child,

I Love You

believe
&
receive

My child,

It is true that in this life you will encounter sorrow and pain. However, do not get discouraged with your current circumstances. Just like the current in the ocean changes so will your current circumstances. I have made a way for you to endure through these times. Trust me and believe that I am working all things in your life for your good.

I Love You ~♥~

Philippians 2:27 (AMP)
He certainly was sick and close to death. But God had mercy on him, and not only on him but also on me, so that I would not have sorrow upon sorrow.

Matthew 26:38-39 (NLT)
He told them, "My soul is crushed with grief to the point of death. Stay here and keep watch with me." 39 He went on a little farther and bowed with his face to the ground, praying, "My Father! If it is possible, let this cup of suffering be taken away from me. Yet I want your will to be done, not mine."

1 Peter 1:6-7 (ESV)
In this you rejoice, though now for a little while, if necessary, you have been grieved by various trials, 7 so that the tested genuineness of your faith—more precious than gold that perishes though it is tested by fire—may be found to result in praise and glory and honor at the revelation of Jesus,

Isaiah 35:10 (HCSB)
...and the redeemed of the Lord will return and come to Zion with singing, crowned with unending joy. Joy and gladness will overtake them, and sorrow and sighing will flee.

John 16:19-20 (MSG)
Jesus knew they were dying to ask him what he meant, so he said, "Are you trying to figure out among yourselves what I meant when I said, 'In a day or so you're not going to see me, but then in another day or so you will see me'? Then fix this firmly in your minds: You're going to be in deep mourning while the godless world throws a party. You'll be sad, very sad, but your sadness will develop into gladness."

My child,

In my presence you will have complete peace. Even when everything is closing in on you, my peace will surround you. Your life can be a testimony to others who watch you walk through turmoil, and remain in my peace. Stay close to me and abide in my presence. Peace is here!

I Love You ~♥~

Isaiah 26:3,12 (NLT)
You will keep in perfect peace all who trust in you, all whose thoughts are fixed on you!
12 Lord, you will grant us peace; all we have accomplished is really from you.

John 14:27 (AMP)
Peace I leave with you; My [perfect] peace I give to you; not as the world gives do I give to you. Do not let your heart be troubled, nor let it be afraid. [Let My perfect peace calm you in every circumstance and give you courage and strength for every challenge.]

2 Thessalonians 3:16 (KJV)
Now the Lord of peace himself give you peace always by all means. The Lord be with you all.

Romans 14:17-19 (ESV)
For the kingdom of God is not a matter of eating and drinking but of righteousness and peace and joy in the Holy Spirit. 18 Whoever thus serves Christ is acceptable to God and approved by men. 19 So then let us pursue what makes for peace and for mutual upbuilding.

My child,

Do not declare death over your life. Through your words you are either speaking death or life - there is no middle ground. Take time and truly listen to yourself. I want you to hear what you are speaking over your life. You may realize what is coming forth from your life begins with what is coming out of your mouth. Speak life and live the life I've purposed for you.

I Love You ~♥~

Isaiah 55:11 (KJV)
So shall my word be that goeth forth out of my mouth: it shall not return unto me void, but it shall accomplish that which I please, and it shall prosper in the thing whereto I sent it.

Ezekiel 12:25 (ESV)
For I am the Lord; I will speak the word that I will speak, and it will be performed. It will no longer be delayed, but in your days, O rebellious house, I will speak the word and perform it, declares the Lord God."

Deuteronomy 30:15-20 (NIV)
See, I set before you today life and prosperity, death and destruction. 16 For I command you today to love the LORD your God, to walk in obedience to him, and to keep his commands, decrees and laws; then you will live and increase, and the LORD your God will bless you in the land you are entering to possess. But if your heart turns away and you are not obedient, and if you are drawn away to bow down to other gods and worship them, I declare to you this day that you will certainly be destroyed. You will not live long in the land you are crossing the Jordan to enter and possess. This day I call the heavens and the earth as witnesses against you that I have set before you life and death, blessings and curses. Now choose life, so that you and your children may live and that you may love the LORD your God, listen to his voice, and hold fast to him. For the LORD is your life, and he will give you many years in the land he swore to give to your fathers, Abraham, Isaac and Jacob.

My child,
You are holding on too tightly to worldly things. I am asking you to let go and take hold of my hand. Total dependency on me requires removing all other obstacles. You build better faith on my foundation.

I Love You ~♥~

1 John 2:15-17 (NLT)
Do not love this world nor the things it offers you, for when you love the world, you do not have the love of the Father in you. 16 For the world offers only a craving for physical pleasure, a craving for everything we see, and pride in our achievements and possessions. These are not from the Father, but are from this world. 17 And this world is fading away, along with everything that people crave. But anyone who does what pleases God will live forever.

1 Peter 1:13-14 (AMP)
So prepare your minds for action, be completely sober [in spirit—steadfast, self-disciplined, spiritually and morally alert], fix your hope completely on the grace [of God] that is coming to you when Jesus Christ is revealed. 14 [Live] as obedient children [of God]; do not be conformed to the evil desires which governed you in your ignorance [before you knew the requirements and transforming power of the good news regarding salvation].

1 Corinthians 3:9-15 (MSG)
Or, to put it another way, you are God's house. Using the gift God gave me as a good architect, I designed blueprints; Apollos is putting up the walls. Let each carpenter who comes on the job take care to build on the foundation! Remember, there is only one foundation, the one already laid: Jesus Christ. Take particular care in picking out your building materials. Eventually there is going to be an inspection. If you use cheap or inferior materials, you'll be found out. The inspection will be thorough and rigorous. You won't get by with a thing. If your work passes inspection, fine; if it doesn't, your part of the building will be torn out and started over. But you won't be torn out; you'll survive—but just barely.

My child,

Do not fear man. I am with you. I go before you and make the path clear for you. I surround you with my protective shields. Place your trust in me, not man. Fear and faith cannot abide in the same vessel. You will bow to one or the other. Surrender your entire life to me, stand on my word, and you will not waver in this world.

I Love You ~♥~

Proverbs 29:25 (MSG)
The fear of human opinion disables; trusting in God protects you from that.

Psalm 27:1 (AMP)
The Lord is my light and my salvation— Whom shall I fear? The Lord is the refuge and fortress of my life— Whom shall I dread?

Psalm 118:5-8 (ESV)
Out of my distress I called on the Lord; the Lord answered me and set me free. 6 The Lord is on my side; I will not fear. What can man do to me? 7 The Lord is on my side as my helper; I shall look in triumph on those who hate me. 8 It is better to take refuge in the Lord than to trust in man.

Deuteronomy 31:6 (HCSB)
Be strong and courageous; don't be terrified or afraid of them. For it is the Lord your God who goes with you; He will not leave you or forsake you."

Psalm 121:8 (KJV)
The Lord shall preserve thy going out and thy coming in from this time forth, and even for evermore.

2 Thessalonians 3:3 (NASB)
But the Lord is faithful, and He will strengthen and protect you from the evil one.

Revelation 3:10 (NLT)
"Because you have obeyed my command to persevere, I will protect you from the great time of testing that will come upon the whole world to test those who belong to this world."

My Child,

I Love You

bring it to the light & God will make it right

My child,

There are mysteries in life that must remain. It will all make sense when we are together face-to-face. But in the meantime, I ask you to trust me without boundaries or borders. I will bless your faith. The more you seek me the freer you become. I do have all the answers to your questions. Will you trust me even if I don't share them with you?

I Love You ~♥~

1 Corinthians 2:7 (NLT)
No, the wisdom we speak of is the mystery of God—his plan that was previously hidden, even though he made it for our ultimate glory before the world began.

Job 11:7 (AMP)
Can you discover the depths of God? Can you [by searching] discover the limits of the Almighty [ascend to His heights, extend to His widths, and comprehend His infinite perfection]?

Colossians 2:2 (ESV)
...that their hearts may be encouraged, being knit together in love, to reach all the riches of full assurance of understanding and the knowledge of God's mystery, which is Christ,

Deuteronomy 29:29 (HCSB)
The hidden things belong to the Lord our God, but the revealed things belong to us and our children forever, so that we may follow all the words of this law.

Ephesians 3:19 (NASB)
...and to know the love of Christ which surpasses knowledge, that you may be filled up to all the fullness of God.

1 Samuel 2:3 (KJV)
Talk no more so exceeding proudly; let not arrogancy come out of your mouth: for the Lord is a God of knowledge, and by him actions are weighed.

My child,

I will always protect the innocent. When you are facing accusation brought on by false information, without hesitation I will bring vindication! I will fight for you and restore honor to your name.

I Love you ~♥~

Isaiah 54:17 (NKJV)
No weapon formed against you shall prosper, And every tongue which rises against you in judgment You shall condemn. This is the heritage of the servants of the Lord, And their righteousness is from Me," Says the Lord.

Psalm 34:7 (ESV)
The angel of the Lord encamps around those who fear him, and delivers them.

2 Timothy 3:10-13 (MSG)
You've been a good apprentice to me, a part of my teaching, my manner of life, direction, faith, steadiness, love, patience, troubles, sufferings—suffering along with me in all the grief I had to put up with in Antioch, Iconium, and Lystra. And you also well know that God rescued me! Anyone who wants to live all out for Christ is in for a lot of trouble; there's no getting around it. Unscrupulous con men will continue to exploit the faith. They're as deceived as the people they lead astray. As long as they are out there, things can only get worse.

Psalm 135:14 (ESV)
For the Lord will vindicate his people and have compassion on his servants.

1 Peter 5:5-7 (NLT)
In the same way, you who are younger must accept the authority of the elders. And all of you, dress yourselves in humility as you relate to one another, for "God opposes the proud but gives grace to the humble." 6 So humble yourselves under the mighty power of God, and at the right time he will lift you up in honor. 7 Give all your worries and cares to God, for he cares about you.

My child,

It is the enemy of your soul that plans to render you useless for my Kingdom. He knows he is defeated! You have been allowing him access through your thoughts. He will play mind games with your thoughts - he wants to convince you that you have no value in my Kingdom. If you will place my protective shield of faith over your mind and give him no territory, your thoughts will be free!

I Love You ~♥~

1 Peter 4:15-16 (AMP)
Make sure that none of you suffers as a murderer, or a thief, or any sort of criminal [in response to persecution], or as a troublesome meddler interfering in the affairs of others; 16 but if anyone suffers [ill-treatment] as a Christian [because of his belief], he is not to be ashamed, but is to glorify God [because he is considered worthy to suffer] in this name.

Ephesians 5:15-17 (HCSB)
Pay careful attention, then, to how you walk—not as unwise people but as wise— 16 making the most of the time, because the days are evil. 17 So don't be foolish, but understand what the Lord's will is.

Romans 13:14 (NLT)
Instead, clothe yourself with the presence of the Lord Jesus Christ. And don't let yourself think about ways to indulge your evil desires.

John 8:47 (NASB)
"He who is of God hears the words of God; for this reason you do not hear them, because you are not of God."

Ephesians 5:15-17 (NLT)
So be careful how you live. Don't live like fools, but like those who are wise. 16 Make the most of every opportunity in these evil days. 17 Don't act thoughtlessly, but understand what the Lord wants you to do.

My child,

You are striving through every day and carrying burdens that I do not intend on you carrying. You are called to abide in me, to cast your burdens and not fret over the things in this life. I paid the price for your peace. It does not cost you anything to have it, but it costs you everything when you lose it. Embrace my peace.

I Love You~♥~

Proverbs 13:10 (AMP)
Through pride and presumption come nothing but strife,
But [skillful and godly] wisdom is with those who welcome [well-advised]
counsel.

2 Timothy 2:22-23 (KJV)
Flee also youthful lusts: but follow righteousness, faith, charity, peace, with them that call on the Lord out of a pure heart. 23 But foolish and unlearned questions avoid, knowing that they do gender strifes.

Philippians 4:6-7 (HCSB)
Don't worry about anything, but in everything, through prayer and petition with thanksgiving, let your requests be made known to God. 7 And the peace of God, which surpasses every thought, will guard your hearts and minds in Christ Jesus.

Isaiah 53:2-6 (MSG)
The servant grew up before God—a scrawny seedling, a scrubby plant in a parched field. There was nothing attractive about him, nothing to cause us to take a second look. He was looked down on and passed over, a man who suffered, who knew pain firsthand. One look at him and people turned away. We looked down on him, thought he was scum. But the fact is, it was our pains he carried— our disfigurements, all the things wrong with us. We thought he brought it on himself, that God was punishing him for his own failures. But it was our sins that did that to him, that ripped and tore and crushed him—our sins! He took the punishment, and that made us whole. Through his bruises we get healed.We're all like sheep who've wandered off and gotten lost. We've all done our own thing, gone our own way. And God has piled all our sins, everything we've done wrong, on him, on him.

My child,
When will you totally trust me? Have I not been deemed trustworthy through your life? Have I not proven to you time and time again that I love you and that I'm a good Father? You waste so much of your peace of mind worrying about many things that will never come to pass. If you would spend the same amount of time in worship as you do in worry; you will be amazed at the peace you will find, and the things of this world will not have an effect on you.

I Love You ~♥~

2 Samuel 7:28-29 (MSG)
"And now, Master God, being the God you are, speaking sure words as you do, and having just said this wonderful thing to me, please, just one more thing: Bless my family; keep your eye on them always. You've already as much as said that you would, Master God! Oh, may your blessing be on my family permanently!"

Jeremiah 7:8-10 (ESV)
"Behold, you trust in deceptive words to no avail. 9 Will you steal, murder, commit adultery, swear falsely, make offerings to Baal, and go after other gods that you have not known, 10 and then come and stand before me in this house, which is called by my name, and say, 'We are delivered!'—only to go on doing all these abominations?"

Daniel 6:23 (HCSB)
The king was overjoyed and gave orders to take Daniel out of the den. So
Daniel was taken out of the den, uninjured, for he trusted in his God.

Romans 15:13 (NLT)
I pray that God, the source of hope, will fill you completely with joy and peace because you trust in him. Then you will overflow with confident hope through the power of the Holy Spirit.

My Child,

_____

_____

_____

_____

_____

_____

_____

_____

_____

_____

_____

_____

_____

_____

_____

_____

_____

_____

_____

_____

_____

_____

_____

_____

_____

_____

_____

I Love You

~ ~

My child,

I am a God of divine order. I do not operate in confusion. When you are in the midst of confusion, take a step back and ask me to reveal the root to you. I will show you where the truth lies. Anything that does not align with my word needs to be detached from your life. My truth brings freedom; not bondage.

I Love You ~♥~

1 John 4:1 (NKJV)
Beloved, do not believe every spirit, but test the spirits, whether they are of God; because many false prophets have gone out into the world.

2 Timothy 3:16-17 (NLT)
All Scripture is inspired by God and is useful to teach us what is true and to make us realize what is wrong in our lives. It corrects us when we are wrong and teaches us to do what is right. 17 God uses it to prepare and equip his people to do every good work.

Proverbs 30:5 (NASB)
Every word of God is tested; He is a shield to those who take refuge in Him.

Deuteronomy 32:4 (HCSB)
The Rock—His work is perfect; all His ways are entirely just. A faithful God, without prejudice, He is righteous and true.

John 16:13 (NIV)
But when he, the Spirit of truth, comes, he will guide you into all the truth. He will not speak on his own; he will speak only what he hears, and he will tell you what is yet to come.

Matthew 7:7-11 (MSG)
"Don't bargain with God. Be direct. Ask for what you need. This isn't a cat-and-mouse, hide-and-seek game we're in. If your child asks for bread, do you trick him with sawdust? If he asks for fish, do you scare him with a live snake on his plate? As bad as you are, you wouldn't think of such a thing. You're at least decent to your own children. So don't you think the God who conceived you in love will be even better?

My child,

Remember that in order, first things have to be first. You will find my favor throughout your day if you will dedicate the first moments of your day to me. Giving your first fruits will bring my favor over your finances. Honor me above all else, let me have first place in your life. I am asking you to examine your heart and rearrange those things that come before me. Be honest with yourself and make the necessary adjustments.

I Love You ~♥~

Exodus 20:3-6 (AMP)
"You shall have no other gods before Me. "You shall not make for yourself any idol, or any likeness (form, manifestation) of what is in heaven above or on the earth beneath or in the water under the earth [as an object to worship]. You shall not worship them nor serve them; for I, the Lord your God, am a jealous (impassioned) God demanding what is rightfully and uniquely mine], visiting (avenging) the iniquity (sin, guilt) of the fathers on the children [that is, calling the children to account for the sins of their fathers], to the third and fourth generations of those who hate Me, but showing graciousness and steadfast lovingkindness to thousands [of generations] of those who love Me and keep My commandments.

Matthew 6:24 (MSG)
"You can't worship two gods at once. Loving one god, you'll end up hating the other. Adoration of one feeds contempt for the other. You can't worship God and Money both.

Colossians 3:23-24 (HCSB)
Whatever you do, do it enthusiastically, as something done for the Lord and not for men, knowing that you will receive the reward of an inheritance from the Lord. You serve the Lord Christ.

Acts 17:28-30 (NLT)
For in him we live and move and exist. As some of your own poets have said, 'We are his offspring.' And since this is true, we shouldn't think of God as an idol designed by craftsmen from gold or silver or stone. "God overlooked people's ignorance about these things in earlier times, but now he commands everyone everywhere to repent of their sins and turn to him.

My child,

Your emptiness cannot be filled by worldly means. Each time you reach for the enticing things of this world you will be empty. There are many counterfeits to be aware of in this life. Seek me for your satisfaction - I will fill you up with amazing joy and you will know the contentment of being filled by my Spirit.

I Love You ~♥~

Isaiah 55:2 (AMP)
"Why do you spend money for that which is not bread, And your earnings for what does not satisfy? Listen carefully to Me, and eat what is good, And let your soul delight in abundance.

Haggai 1:5-6 (ESV)
Now, therefore, thus says the Lord of hosts: Consider your ways. 6 You have sown much, and harvested little. You eat, but you never have enough; you drink, but you never have your fill. You clothe yourselves, but no one is warm. And he who earns wages does so to put them into a bag with holes.

Psalm 81:10 (HCSB)
I am Yahweh your God, who brought you up from the land of Egypt.
Open your mouth wide, and I will fill it.

John 1:16 (KJV)
And of his fulness have all we received, and grace for grace.

John 10:6-10 (MSG)
Jesus told this simple story, but they had no idea what he was talking about. So he tried again. "I'll be explicit, then. I am the Gate for the sheep. All those others are up to no good—sheep stealers, every one of them. But the sheep didn't listen to them. I am the Gate. Anyone who goes through me will be cared for— will freely go in and out, and find pasture. A thief is only there to steal and kill and destroy. I came so they can have real and eternal life, more and better life than they ever dreamed of.

My child,

Where is your heart? What do you treasure in this life? The world measures value differently than I. What do you value? Is it possessions, power, positions, prestige? I place value on people. Today take an assessment and ask yourself what is valuable to you? One way to determine what you value; look at how you spend your time. Make people a priority.

I Love You ~♥~

Matthew 6:19-21 (MSG)
"Don't hoard treasure down here where it gets eaten by moths and corroded by rust or—worse!—stolen by burglars. Stockpile treasure in heaven, where it's safe from moth and rust and burglars. It's obvious, isn't it? The place where your treasure is, is the place you will most want to be, and end up being."

Philippians 3:8-9 (AMP)
But more than that, I count everything as loss compared to the priceless privilege and supreme advantage of knowing Christ Jesus my Lord [and of growing more deeply and thoroughly acquainted with Him—a joy unequaled]. For His sake I have lost everything, and I consider it all garbage, so that I may gain Christ, 9 and may be found in Him [believing and relying on Him], not having any righteousness of my own derived from [my obedience to] the Law and its rituals, but [possessing] that [genuine righteousness] which comes through faith in Christ, the righteousness which comes from God on the basis of faith.

James 3:13-17 (NLT)
If you are wise and understand God's ways, prove it by living an honorable life, doing good works with the humility that comes from wisdom. 14 But if you are bitterly jealous and there is selfish ambition in your heart, don't cover up the truth with boasting and lying. 15 For jealousy and selfishness are not God's kind of wisdom. Such things are earthly, unspiritual, and demonic. 16 For wherever there is jealousy and selfish ambition, there you will find disorder and evil of every kind. 17 But the wisdom from above is first of all pure. It is also peace loving, gentle at all times, and willing to yield to others. It is full of mercy and the fruit of good deeds. It shows no favoritism and is always sincere.

My child,

When you abide in me you are never alone. I am near to you. I know each and every beat of your heart. Every breath you take comes from me. I hold your life in my hands. You can rest assured in knowing I am aware of everything in your life. Nothing is hidden from me.

I Love You ~♥~

Isaiah 41:10 (AMP)
'Do not fear [anything], for I am with you; Do not be afraid, for I am your God. I will strengthen you, be assured I will help you; I will certainly take hold of you with My righteous right hand [a hand of justice, of power, of victory, of salvation].'

Deuteronomy 31:8 (ESV)
"It is the Lord who goes before you. He will be with you; he will not leave you or forsake you. Do not fear or be dismayed."

Exodus 33:14 (HCSB)
Then He replied, "My presence will go with you, and I will give you rest."

Psalm 34:17-19 (MSG)
Is anyone crying for help? God is listening, ready to rescue you. 18 If your heart is broken, you'll find God right there; if you're kicked in the gut, he'll help you catch your breath. 19 Disciples so often get into trouble; still, God is there every time.

Psalm 54:4 (KJV)
Behold, God is mine helper: the Lord is with them that uphold my soul.

John 14:27 (NASB)
Peace I leave with you; My peace I give to you; not as the world gives do I give to you. Do not let your heart be troubled, nor let it be fearful.

My Child,

_____

_____

_____

_____

_____

_____

_____

_____

_____

_____

_____

_____

_____

_____

_____

_____

_____

_____

_____

_____

_____

_____

_____

_____

_____

I Love You

~~

My child,
Do you know why you are feeling numb? Could it possibly be that you have protected your heart from others and now you can't feel my Spirit? When you go into self-protection, you are taking matters into your own hands. Ask me to protect you and trust me with the results. I created your heart and who better than I to be the keeper of your heart?

I Love You ~♥~

Psalm 51:7-15 (MSG)
Soak me in your laundry and I'll come out clean, scrub me and I'll have a snow-white life. Tune me in to foot-tapping songs, set these once-broken bones to dancing. Don't look too close for blemishes, give me a clean bill of health. God, make a fresh start in me, shape a Genesis week from the chaos of my life. Don't throw me out with the trash, or fail to breathe holiness in me. Bring me back from gray exile, put a fresh wind in my sails! Give me a job teaching rebels your ways so the lost can find their way home. Commute my death sentence, God, my salvation God, and I'll sing anthems to your life-giving ways. Unbutton my lips, dear God; I'll let loose with your praise.

Psalm 121:5 (ESV)
The Lord is your keeper; the Lord is your shade on your right hand.

2 Timothy 1:12 (AMP)
This is why I suffer as I do. Still, I am not ashamed; for I know Him [and I am personally acquainted with Him] whom I have believed [with absolute trust and confidence in Him and in the truth of His deity], and I am persuaded [beyond any doubt] that He is able to guard that which I have entrusted to Him until that day [when I stand before Him].

Psalm 37:3 (HCSB)
Trust in the Lord and do what is good; dwell in the land and live securely.

My child,

You are free to run within my boundaries and borders. As you abide with me, you will experience true freedom. When you move yourself outside of my boundaries and borders, you are entering the enemy's territory. In this territory, you become susceptible to deception and attacks. There is safety with me. Stay in the boundaries of my word and ways.

I Love You ~♥~

Psalm 74:16-17 (AMP)
The day is Yours, the night also is Yours; You have established and prepared the [heavenly] light and the sun. 17 You have defined and established all the borders of the earth [the divisions of land and sea and of the nations]; You have made summer and winter.

Exodus 23:31 (ESV)
And I will set your border from the Red Sea to the Sea of the Philistines, and from the wilderness to the Euphrates, for I will give the inhabitants of the land into your hand, and you shall drive them out before you.

1 Corinthians 10:13 (HCSB)
No temptation has overtaken you except what is common to humanity. God is faithful, and He will not allow you to be tempted beyond what you are able, but with the temptation He will also provide a way of escape so that you are able to bear it.

Psalm 5:11 (KJV)
But let all those that put their trust in thee rejoice: let them ever shout for joy, because thou defendest them: let them also that love thy name be joyful in thee.

Psalm 138:7-8 (MSG)
When I walk into the thick of trouble, keep me alive in the angry turmoil. With one hand strike my foes, With your other hand save me. Finish what you started in me, God. Your love is eternal—don't quit on me now.

My child,

You are called to serve one another. When you look past your struggles to strengthen another, you will find strength. When you provide financially for others, you will never lack anything in life. If in your sorrow, you can rejoice with others, I will bless you with unspeakable joy in your heart. You being a servant to others is a blessing to me.

I Love You ~♥~

Matthew 23:10-12 (AMP)
Do not let yourselves be called leaders or teachers; for One is your Leader (Teacher), the Christ. 11 But the greatest among you will be your servant. 12 Whoever exalts himself shall be humbled; and whoever humbles himself shall be raised to honor.

Luke 6:38 (ESV)
...give, and it will be given to you. Good measure, pressed down, shaken together, running over, will be put into your lap. For with the measure you use it will be measured back to you."

Galatians 6:9-10 (MSG)
So let's not allow ourselves to get fatigued doing good. At the right time we will harvest a good crop if we don't give up, or quit. Right now, therefore, every time we get the chance, let us work for the benefit of all, starting with the people closest to us in the community of faith.

Colossians 3:23-24 (NLT)
Work willingly at whatever you do, as though you were working for the Lord rather than for people. 24 Remember that the Lord will give you an inheritance as your reward, and that the Master you are serving is Christ.

1 Peter 1:7-9 (KJV)
That the trial of your faith, being much more precious than of gold that perisheth, though it be tried with fire, might be found unto praise and honour and glory at the appearing of Jesus Christ: 8 Whom having not seen, ye love; in whom, though now ye see him not, yet believing, ye rejoice with joy unspeakable and full of glory: 9 Receiving the end of your faith, even the salvation of your souls.

My child,

The judgment of the world is in my hands. You are not going to have peace in your life while you live in judgement of this world. It is true that you will not find comfort and peace within the world. Why are you surprised at the Godless ways of the world? As my child, you are in a foreign land - you won't be able to understand the language of this world. Let go of your offense at the world, stop judging and start loving the millions of people that are lost and going to hell. Love will bring them home.

I Love You ~♥~

Acts 17:30-31 (NIV)
"In the past God overlooked such ignorance, but now he commands all people everywhere to repent. 31 For he has set a day when he will judge the world with justice by the man he has appointed. He has given proof of this to everyone by raising him from the dead."

1 Peter 2:11-12 (MSG)
Friends, this world is not your home, so don't make yourselves cozy in it. Don't indulge your ego at the expense of your soul. Live an exemplary life among the natives so that your actions will refute their prejudices. Then they'll be won over to God's side and be there to join in the celebration when he arrives.

Hebrews 13:14-16 (NLT)
For this world is not our permanent home; we are looking forward to a home yet to come. 15 Therefore, let us offer through Jesus a continual sacrifice of praise to God, proclaiming our allegiance to his name. 16 And don't forget to do good and to share with those in need. These are the sacrifices that please God.

Proverbs 9:7-9 (AMP)
He who corrects and instructs a scoffer gets dishonor for himself, And he who rebukes a wicked man gets insults for himself. 8 Do not correct a scoffer [who foolishly ridicules and takes no responsibility for his error] or he will hate you; Correct a wise man [who learns from his error], and he will love you. 9 Give instruction to a wise man and he will become even wiser; Teach a righteous man and he will increase his learning.

My child,

Today I want you to count your blessings. Even in the midst of uncertain times, you are blessed. As you recall the blessings, take time to speak out your gratitude to me and others around you. Having gratitude keeps away a bad attitude. Do not allow the enemy to take your praise!

I Love You ♥

Deuteronomy 28:1-6 (MSG)
If you listen obediently to the Voice of God, your God, and heartily obey all his commandments that I command you today, God, your God, will place you on high, high above all the nations of the world. All these blessings will come down on you and spread out beyond you because you have responded to the Voice of God, your God: God's blessing inside the city, God's blessing in the country; God's blessing on your children, the crops of your land, the young of your livestock, the calves of your herds, the lambs of your flocks. God's blessing on your basket and bread bowl; God's blessing in your coming in, God's blessing in your going out.

Psalm 105:1 (KJV)
O give thanks unto the Lord; call upon his name: make known his deeds among the people.

Psalm 103:2-5 (AMP)
Bless and affectionately praise the Lord, O my soul, And do not forget any of His benefits; 3 Who forgives all your sins, Who heals all your diseases; 4 Who redeems your life from the pit, Who crowns you [lavishly] with lovingkindness and tender mercy; 5 Who satisfies your years with good things, So that your youth is renewed like the [soaring] eagle.

Philippians 4:8 (HCSB)
Finally brothers, whatever is true, whatever is honorable, whatever is just, whatever is pure, whatever is lovely, whatever is commendable—if there is any moral excellence and if there is any praise—dwell on these things.

Colossians 3:2-4 (NLT)
Think about the things of heaven, not the things of earth. 3 For you died to this life, and your real life is hidden with Christ in God. 4 And when Christ, who is your life, is revealed to the whole world, you will share in all his glory.

300

My Child,

_____

_____

_____

_____

_____

_____

_____

_____

_____

_____

_____

_____

_____

_____

_____

_____

_____

_____

_____

_____

_____

_____

_____

_____

_____

_____

I Love You

~ ~

My child,

My hope truly is the anchor for your soul. You must tether yourself to my hope. The storms of life are ferocious. If you're not attached to the anchor of my hope, you will find yourself tossed to and fro on the sea of despair. Anchor your life in my hope - there is no other place to find grace!

I Love You ~♥~

Hebrews 6:19-20 (ESV)
We have this as a sure and steadfast anchor of the soul, a hope that enters into the inner place behind the curtain, 20 where Jesus has gone as a forerunner on our behalf, having become a high priest forever after the order of Melchizedek.

1 Timothy 6:17 (NLT)
Teach those who are rich in this world not to be proud and not to trust in their money, which is so unreliable. Their trust should be in God, who richly gives us all we need for our enjoyment.

Psalm 27:13-14 (MSG)
I'm sure now I'll see God's goodness in the exuberant earth. Stay with God! Take heart. Don't quit. I'll say it again: Stay with God.

Romans 15:13 (NKJV)
Now may the God of hope fill you with all joy and peace in believing, that you may abound in hope by the power of the Holy Spirit.

My child,

This world is filled with deception. The enemy does not have any new tricks. Just as he planted the seed of deception in Eve with the question, "Did God really mean what he said?", that is what he is doing to you. He wants to separate you from me by getting you to doubt me. My words have never, nor will they ever, change. You can trust me with everything. I am the solid, firm, tried and true foundation you need. Turn your ear away from the enemy and become deaf to deception.

I Love You ~♥~

Genesis 3:1 (NLT)
The serpent was the shrewdest of all the wild animals the Lord God had made. One day he asked the woman, "Did God really say you must not eat the fruit from any of the trees in the garden?"

2 Corinthians 11:3 (AMP)
But I am afraid that, even as the serpent beguiled Eve by his cunning, your minds may be corrupted and led away from the simplicity of [your sincere and] pure devotion to Christ.

1 John 4:1 (NKJV)
Beloved, do not believe every spirit, but test the spirits, whether they are of God; because many false prophets have gone out into the world.

Numbers 23:19 (NIV)
God is not human, that he should lie, not a human being, that he should change his mind. Does he speak and then not act? Does he promise and not fulfill?

James 1:16-18 (MSG)
So, my very dear friends, don't get thrown off course. Every desirable and beneficial gift comes out of heaven. The gifts are rivers of light cascading down from the Father of Light. There is nothing deceitful in God, nothing two-faced, nothing fickle. He brought us to life using the true Word, showing us off as the crown of all his creatures.

My child,

Today I want to lead you beside the still waters and refresh your soul. If you will slow down and make yourself available to me, I will refill your dry thirsty soul. There are no substitutes for my fulfillment. Come today, sit with me, and enjoy sweet fellowship!

I Love You ~♥~

Psalm 23:2-3 (KJV)
He maketh me to lie down in green pastures: he leadeth me beside the still waters. 3 He restoreth my soul: he leadeth me in the paths of righteousness for his name's sake.

Jeremiah 31:25 (AMP)
For I [fully] satisfy the weary soul, and I replenish every languishing and sorrowful person.

Isaiah 58:11 (ESV)
And the Lord will guide you continually and satisfy your desire in scorched places and make your bones strong; and you shall be like a watered garden, like a spring of water, whose waters do not fail.

Psalm 107:9 (HCSB)
For He has satisfied the thirsty and filled the hungry with good things.

1 Corinthians 1:9 (NASB)
God is faithful, through whom you were called into fellowship with His Son, Jesus Christ our Lord.

Luke 24:32 (NLT)
They said to each other, "Didn't our hearts burn within us as he talked with us on the road and explained the Scriptures to us?"

My child,
Many times I've heard you say, "God, where are you?" There is never a question of where I am. You need to ask yourself, "Where am I?" You have discarded me while making decisions or choices. When you choose to do this, you are choosing the consequences that go along with the choices you make. You and I need to be partners. I promise to always do my part...will you do yours?

I Love You ~♥~

Isaiah 41:10 (NLT)
Don't be afraid, for I am with you. Don't be discouraged, for I am your God. I will strengthen you and help you. I will hold you up with my victorious right hand.

John 3:16-18 (NKJV)
For God so loved the world that He gave His only begotten Son, that whoever believes in Him should not perish but have everlasting life. 17 For God did not send His Son into the world to condemn the world, but that the world through Him might be saved. 18 "He who believes in Him is not condemned; but he who does not believe is condemned already, because he has not believed in the name of the only begotten Son of God.

Psalm 73:23-26 (NIV)
Yet I am always with you; you hold me by my right hand. 24 You guide me with your counsel, and afterward you will take me into glory. 25 Whom have I in heaven but you? And earth has nothing I desire besides you. 26 My flesh and my heart may fail, but God is the strength of my heart and my portion forever.

Matthew 11:28-30 (MSG)
"Are you tired? Worn out? Burned out on religion? Come to me. Get away with me and you'll recover your life. I'll show you how to take a real rest. Walk with me and work with me—watch how I do it. Learn the unforced rhythms of grace. I won't lay anything heavy or ill-fitting on you. Keep company with me and you'll learn to live freely and lightly."

My child,

The oppression you are experiencing is coming from unresolved bitterness. The enemy works best through an offended heart. I am asking you today to let go of everything, any event and everyone that has brought hurt to you. IF you will release your expectations of them and place your expectations on me, you will find healing and be released from this oppression. I have called you this day to be healed.

I Love You ~♥~

Psalm 43:1-4 (NIV)
Vindicate me, my God, and plead my cause against an unfaithful nation. Rescue me from those who are deceitful and wicked. 2 You are God my stronghold. Why have you rejected me? Why must I go about mourning, oppressed by the enemy? 3 Send me your light and your faithful care, let them lead me; let them bring me to your holy mountain, to the place where you dwell. 4 Then I will go to the altar of God, to God, my joy and my delight. I will praise you with the lyre, O God, my God.

Luke 6:27-36 (HCSB)
But I say to you who listen: Love your enemies, do what is good to those who hate you, 28 bless those who curse you, pray for those who mistreat you. 29 If anyone hits you on the cheek, offer the other also. And if anyone takes away your coat, don't hold back your shirt either. 30 Give to everyone who asks you, and from one who takes your things, don't ask for them back. 31 Just as you want others to do for you, do the same for them. 32 If you love those who love you, what credit is that to you? Even sinners love those who love them. 33 If you do what is good to those who are good to you, what credit is that to you? Even sinners do that. 34 And if you lend to those from whom you expect to receive, what credit is that to you? Even sinners lend to sinners to be repaid in full. 35 But love your enemies, do what is good, and lend, expecting nothing in return. Then your reward will be great, and you will be sons of the Most High. For He is gracious to the ungrateful and evil. 36 Be merciful, just as your Father also is merciful.

My Child,

I Love You

~ ~

				[3] h	
	[2] d			e	
[1] R	e	v	e	a	l
	a			l	
	l				

My child,

When it is time to respond, you will know what to do. Your anxiousness comes upon you when you're trying to figure out the answers before you need them. When you trust me with all your heart, you will find comfort in not having all the answers, but knowing that I do. I will not leave you lacking. Seek me first, and then everything else will follow.

I Love You ~♥~

Acts 1:7 (ESV)
He said to them, "It is not for you to know times or seasons that the Father has fixed by his own authority.

Ecclesiastes 3:11 (AMP)
He has made everything beautiful and appropriate in its time. He has also planted eternity [a sense of divine purpose] in the human heart [a mysterious longing which nothing under the sun can satisfy, except God]—yet man cannot find out (comprehend, grasp) what God has done (His overall plan) from the beginning to the end.

Matthew 6:25-26 (MSG)
If you decide for God, living a life of God-worship, it follows that you don't fuss about what's on the table at mealtimes or whether the clothes in your closet are in fashion. There is far more to your life than the food you put in your stomach, more to your outer appearance than the clothes you hang on your body. Look at the birds, free and unfettered, not tied down to a job description, careless in the care of God. And you count far more to him than birds.

Proverbs 12:25 (NASB)
Anxiety in a man's heart weighs it down, But a good word makes it glad.

James 1:3-5 (NLT)
For you know that when your faith is tested, your endurance has a chance to grow. 4 So let it grow, for when your endurance is fully developed, you will be perfect and complete, needing nothing. 5 If you need wisdom, ask our generous God, and he will give it to you. He will not rebuke you for asking.

My child,

It's time to change your perspective to a more eternal one. If you will focus your attention upward, these worldly distractions will bother you less. Having an eternal focus brings clarity to a faulty world. Realizing that you are not in control, and truly looking to me is one way to change your perspective.

I Love You ~♥~

James 4:13-17 (NLT)
Look here, you who say, "Today or tomorrow we are going to a certain town and will stay there a year. We will do business there and make a profit." 14 How do you know what your life will be like tomorrow? Your life is like the morning fog—it's here a little while, then it's gone. 15 What you ought to say is, "If the Lord wants us to, we will live and do this or that." 16 Otherwise you are boasting about your own pretentious plans, and all such boasting is evil. 17 Remember, it is sin to know what you ought to do and then not do it.

Psalm 39:4-7 (HCSB)
"Lord, reveal to me the end of my life and the number of my days.
Let me know how short-lived I am. 5 You, indeed, have made my days short in length, and my life span as nothing in Your sight. Yes, every mortal man is only a vapor. Selah. 6 "Certainly, man walks about like a mere shadow. Indeed, they frantically rush around in vain, gathering possessions without knowing who will get them.
7 Now, Lord, what do I wait for? My hope is in You.

Colossians 3:1-2 (AMP)
Therefore if you have been raised with Christ [to a new life, sharing in His resurrection from the dead], keep seeking the things that are above, where Christ is, seated at the right hand of God. 2 Set your mind and keep focused habitually on the things above [the heavenly things], not on things that are on the earth [which have only temporal value].

My child,

You can have a new beginning. You must decide to leave the past in the past and step into a new place with me. You cannot move forward if you continue to drag the past hurts and heartaches with you. Trust me to redeem and restore those areas. You let go and allow me to vindicate and validate you.

I Love You ~♥~

Isaiah 65:17 (KJV)
For, behold, I create new heavens and a new earth: and the former shall not be remembered, nor come into mind.

2 Corinthians 5:17 (AMP)
Therefore if anyone is in Christ [that is, grafted in, joined to Him by faith in Him as Savior], he is a new creature [reborn and renewed by the Holy Spirit]; the old things [the previous moral and spiritual condition] have passed away. Behold, new things have come [because spiritual awakening brings a new life].

Isaiah 43:18-19 (ESV)
"Remember not the former things, nor consider the things of old.
19 Behold, I am doing a new thing; now it springs forth, do you not perceive it? I will make a way in the wilderness and rivers in the desert.

Ephesians 4:22-24 (HCSB)
You took off your former way of life, the old self that is corrupted by deceitful desires; 23 you are being renewed in the spirit of your minds; 24 you put on the new self, the one created according to God's likeness in righteousness and purity of the truth.

Luke 7:47 (NKJV)
Therefore I say to you, her sins, which are many, are forgiven, for she loved much. But to whom little is forgiven, the same loves little."

Revelation 21:5 (NASB)
And He who sits on the throne said, "Behold, I am making all things new." And He *said, "Write, for these words are faithful and true."

My child,

You are going into a transitional season. It may feel like everything is shifting around you, but do not fear. I will bring you back to balance. I am your sure footing and there is no other foundation to build upon but me. Any attempts to build without me will eventually fail you. If you are unsure of the plan, consult with me; I AM the designer of your blueprint.

I Love You ~♥~

Psalm 119:30-32 (NIV)
I have chosen the way of faithfulness; I have set my heart on your laws. 31 I hold fast to your statutes, Lord; do not let me be put to shame. 32 I run in the path of your commands, for you have broadened my understanding.

Titus 3:5-7 (AMP)
He saved us, not because of any works of righteousness that we have done, but because of His own compassion and mercy, by the cleansing of the new birth (spiritual transformation, regeneration) and renewing by the Holy Spirit, 6 whom He poured out richly upon us through Jesus Christ our Savior, 7 so that we would be justified [made free of the guilt of sin] by His [compassionate, undeserved] grace, and that we would be [acknowledged as acceptable to Him and] made heirs of eternal life [actually experiencing it] according to our hope (His guarantee).

1 Corinthians 3:9-15 (MSG)
Or, to put it another way, you are God's house. Using the gift God gave me as a good architect, I designed blueprints; Apollos is putting up the walls. Let each carpenter who comes on the job take care to build on the foundation! Remember, there is only one foundation, the one already laid: Jesus Christ. Take particular care in picking out your building materials. Eventually there is going to be an inspection. If you use cheap or inferior materials, you'll be found out. The inspection will be thorough and rigorous. You won't get by with a thing. If your work passes inspection, fine; if it doesn't, your part of the building will be torn out and started over. But you won't be torn out; you'll survive—but just barely.

My child,
As you are stepping into unfamiliar territory, do not fear what is ahead of you. I've told you in my word that I go before you, now trust me with all your heart. I am in this very moment supplying all that you need to succeed. When you stay true to who I've created you to be, all they will see is me!

I Love You ~♥~

Isaiah 42:16 (NIV)
I will lead the blind by ways they have not known, along unfamiliar paths I will guide them; I will turn the darkness into light before them and make the rough places smooth. These are the things I will do; I will not forsake them.

1 Chronicles 4:10 (NLT)
He was the one who prayed to the God of Israel, "Oh, that you would bless me and expand my territory! Please be with me in all that I do, and keep me from all trouble and pain!" And God granted him his request.

Ephesians 3:17-19 (AMP)
...so that Christ may dwell in your hearts through your faith. And may you, having been [deeply] rooted and [securely] grounded in love, 18 be fully capable of comprehending with all the saints (God's people) the width and length and height and depth of His love [fully experiencing that amazing, endless love]; 19 and [that you may come] to know [practically, through personal experience] the love of Christ which far surpasses [mere] knowledge [without experience], that you may be filled up [throughout your being] to all the fullness of God [so that you may have the richest experience of God's presence in your lives, completely filled and flooded with God Himself].

Proverbs 2:6-8 (MSG)
And here's why: God gives out Wisdom free, is plainspoken in Knowledge and Understanding. He's a rich mine of Common Sense for those who live well, a personal bodyguard to the candid and sincere. He keeps his eye on all who live honestly, and pays special attention to his loyally committed ones.

My Child,

_____
_____
_____
_____
_____
_____
_____
_____
_____
_____
_____
_____
_____
_____
_____
_____
_____
_____
_____
_____
_____
_____
_____
_____
_____
_____
_____
_____

I Love You

~~

abide

DONT STRIVE

My child,

The time is here for you to stand alone. No longer will you prop yourself up, it's time to stand! The past months have been a testing time of endurance. It is time for you to stand for yourself. I am with you. And you with me. Together we are strong enough. This stand-alone time will show others that your strength truly comes through me.

I Love You ~♥~

1 Corinthians 15:58(NASB)
Therefore, my beloved brethren, be steadfast, immovable, always abounding in the work of the Lord, knowing that your toil is not in vain in the Lord.

Galatians 5:1 (AMP)
It was for this freedom that Christ set us free [completely liberating us]; therefore keep standing firm and do not be subject again to a yoke of slavery [which you once removed].

James 1:2-4 (HCSB)
Consider it a great joy, my brothers, whenever you experience various trials, 3 knowing that the testing of your faith produces endurance. 4 But endurance must do its complete work, so that you may be mature and complete, lacking nothing.

Luke 9:57-62(MSG)
On the road someone asked if he could go along. "I'll go with you, wherever," he said. 58 Jesus was curt: "Are you ready to rough it? We're not staying in the best inns, you know." Jesus said to another, "Follow me." 59 He said, "Certainly, but first excuse me for a couple of days, please. I have to make arrangements for my father's funeral." 60 Jesus refused. "First things first. Your business is life, not death. And life is urgent: Announce God's kingdom!" 61 Then another said, "I'm ready to follow you, Master, but first excuse me while I get things straightened out at home." 62 Jesus said, "No procrastination. No backward looks. You can't put God's kingdom off till tomorrow. Seize the day."

My child,

I have called you out of the darkness into the marvelous light. No longer do you dwell in the darkness of past decisions. You are redeemed and the blood of Jesus renews your life through the power of the resurrection. Live in the light of my love. The light exposes every area of deception and brings deliverance.

I Love You ~♥~

Colossians 1:12-14 (AMP)
12 giving thanks to the Father, who has qualified us to share in the inheritance of the saints (God's people) in the Light. 13 For He has rescued us and has drawn us to Himself from the dominion of darkness, and has transferred us to the kingdom of His beloved Son, 14 in whom we have redemption [because of His sacrifice, resulting in] the forgiveness of our sins [and the cancellation of sins' penalty].

1 Peter 2:9 (ESV)
But you are a chosen race, a royal priesthood, a holy nation, a people for his own possession, that you may proclaim the excellencies of him who called you out of darkness into his marvelous light.

Ephesians 1:6-9 (HCSB)
to the praise of His glorious grace that He favored us with in the Beloved. 7 We have redemption in Him through His blood, the forgiveness of our trespasses, according to the riches of His grace 8 that He lavished on us with all wisdom and understanding. 9 He made known to us the mystery of His will, according to His good pleasure that He planned in Him.

Romans 3:25-26 (KJV)
Whom God hath set forth to be a propitiation through faith in his blood, to declare his righteousness for the remission of sins that are past, through the forbearance of God; 26 To declare, I say, at this time his righteousness: that he might be just, and the justifier of him which believeth in Jesus.

John 8:12 (MSG)
Jesus once again addressed them: "I am the world's Light. No one who follows me stumbles around in the darkness. I provide plenty of light to live in."

My child,

Clear your mind of clutter. Your thoughts drive your life. You must resist reckless thoughts; this only leads to damage. Exchange your turmoil-filled thoughts for my peace that surpasses your own understanding. I proclaim to you today, that through me you are victorious. Think good thoughts, and keep your mind on your own business.

I Love You ~♥~

1 Corinthians 2:13-16 (AMP)
We also speak of these things, not in words taught or supplied by human wisdom, but in those taught by the Spirit, combining and interpreting spiritual thoughts with spiritual words [for those being guided by the Holy Spirit]. 14 But the natural [unbelieving] man does not accept the things [the teachings and revelations] of the Spirit of God, for they are foolishness [absurd and illogical] to him; and he is incapable of understanding them, because they are spiritually discerned and appreciated, [and he is unqualified to judge spiritual matters]. 15 But the spiritual man [the spiritually mature Christian] judges all things [questions, examines and applies what the Holy Spirit reveals], yet is himself judged by no one [the unbeliever cannot judge and understand the believer's spiritual nature]. 16 For who has known the mind and purposes of the Lord, so as to instruct Him? But we have the mind of Christ [to be guided by His thoughts and purposes].

2 Timothy 1:7 (KJV)
For God hath not given us the spirit of fear; but of power, and of love, and of a sound mind.

Philippians 2:5-8 (NIV)
In your relationships with one another, have the same mindset as Christ Jesus: 6 Who, being in very nature God, did not consider equality with God something to be used to his own advantage; 7 rather, he made himself nothing by taking the very nature of a servant, being made in human likeness. 8 And being found in appearance as a man, he humbled himself by becoming obedient to death— even death on a cross!

My child,
The pressure you are enduring is making your stronger. Look up and lean on me for direction and protection. Abide in my presence and trust me to navigate you through this difficult season. Just as the seed planted in the ground has to endure pressure to reach the harvest, so must you. Wait just a little while - harvest time is near!

I Love You ~♥~

James 1:2-4 (MSG)
Consider it a sheer gift, friends, when tests and challenges come at you from all sides. You know that under pressure, your faith-life is forced into the open and shows its true colors. So don't try to get out of anything prematurely. Let it do its work so you become mature and well-developed, not deficient in any way.

Isaiah 41:10 (AMP)
'Do not fear [anything], for I am with you; Do not be afraid, for I am your God. I will strengthen you, be assured I will help you; I will certainly take hold of you with My righteous right hand [a hand of justice, of power, of victory, of salvation]."

John 16:33 (ESV)
"I have said these things to you, that in me you may have peace. In the world you will have tribulation. But take heart; I have overcome the world."

2 Corinthians 4:16-18 (HCSB)
Therefore we do not give up. Even though our outer person is being destroyed, our inner person is being renewed day by day. 17 For our momentary light affliction[a] is producing for us an absolutely incomparable eternal weight of glory. 18 So we do not focus on what is seen, but on what is unseen. For what is seen is temporary, but what is unseen is eternal.

Psalm 46:1 (KJV)
God is our refuge and strength, a very present help in trouble.

My child,

Bring your brokenness to me. I am the divine healer. Invite me into your wounded areas and give me full access to your heart. I will completely heal and restore you. I cannot change what happened to you in the past, but my healing will change you and how you view the past. Trust me to turn past burdens into present blessings.

I Love You ~♥~

Isaiah 57:14-21 (ESV)
And it shall be said, "Build up, build up, prepare the way, remove every obstruction from my people's way." 15 For thus says the One who is high and lifted up, who inhabits eternity, whose name is Holy: "I dwell in the high and holy place, and also with him who is of a contrite and lowly spirit, to revive the spirit of the lowly, and to revive the heart of the contrite. 16 For I will not contend forever, nor will I always be angry; for the spirit would grow faint before me, and the breath of life that I made. 17 Because of the iniquity of his unjust gain I was angry, I struck him; I hid my face and was angry, but he went on backsliding in the way of his own heart. 18 I have seen his ways, but I will heal him; I will lead him and restore comfort to him and his mourners, 19 creating the fruit of the lips. Peace, peace, to the far and to the near," says the Lord, "and I will heal him. 20 But the wicked are like the tossing sea; for it cannot be quiet, and its waters toss up mire and dirt. 21 There is no peace," says my God, "for the wicked."

Psalm 34:18 (AMP)
The Lord is near to the heartbroken And He saves those who are crushed in spirit (contrite in heart, truly sorry for their sin).

2 Corinthians 5:17-18 (NIV)
Therefore, if anyone is in Christ, the new creation has come: The old has gone, the new is here! 18 All this is from God, who reconciled us to himself through Christ and gave us the ministry of reconciliation:

My Child,

_____

_____

_____

_____

_____

_____

_____

_____

_____

_____

_____

_____

_____

_____

_____

_____

_____

_____

_____

_____

_____

_____

_____

_____

_____

_____

I Love You

~ ~

you've got to FEEL it to heal it

My *child,*
In this life you will encounter opposition. Be alert and ready at all times because the enemy is continuously plotting your demise. Do not shrink back in fear. In moments of opposition; stand in faith and rise up in boldness. Greater is he in you than he that is in this world. You are made stronger through resistance.

I Love You ~♥~

Psalm 37:1-6 (ESV)
Fret not yourself because of evildoers; be not envious of wrongdoers! 2 For they will soon fade like the grass and wither like the green herb. 3 Trust in the Lord, and do good; dwell in the land and befriend faithfulness. 4 Delight yourself in the Lord, and he will give you the desires of your heart. 5 Commit your way to the Lord; trust in him, and he will act. 6 He will bring forth your righteousness as the light, and your justice as the noonday.

Deuteronomy 20:1 (NIV)
When you go to war against your enemies and see horses and chariots and an army greater than yours, do not be afraid of them, because the Lord your God, who brought you up out of Egypt, will be with you.

Exodus 23:22 (HCSB)
But if you will carefully obey him and do everything I say, then I will be an enemy to your enemies and a foe to your foes.

1 Corinthians 16:13 (NLT)
Be on guard. Stand firm in the faith. Be courageous. Be strong.

Psalm 27:14 (KJV)
Wait on the Lord: be of good courage, and he shall strengthen thine heart: wait, I say, on the Lord.

1 John 4:4 (NIV)
You, dear children, are from God and have overcome them, because the one who is in you is greater than the one who is in the world.

My child,

Today I am returning dignity to you. I am making you clean, in every area where you have felt disgusted, dirty or damaged. I AM, the Great I AM, and I speak to you today...no longer are you a slave to shame; you are righteous and redeemed! Believe me - You are free!

I Love You ~♥~

1 Samuel 2:6-10 (MSG)
God brings death and God brings life, brings down to the grave and raises up. God brings poverty and God brings wealth; he lowers, he also lifts up. He puts poor people on their feet again; he rekindles burned-out lives with fresh hope, Restoring dignity and respect to their lives— a place in the sun! For the very structures of earth are God's; he has laid out his operations on a firm foundation. He protectively cares for his faithful friends, step by step, but leaves the wicked to stumble in the dark. No one makes it in this life by sheer muscle! God's enemies will be blasted out of the sky, crashed in a heap and burned. God will set things right all over the earth, he'll give strength to his king, he'll set his anointed on top of the world!

Jeremiah 1:5 (AMP)
"Before I formed you in the womb I knew you [and approved of you as My chosen instrument], And before you were born I consecrated you [to Myself as My own]; I have appointed you as a prophet to the nations."

John 10:10 (ESV)
The thief comes only to steal and kill and destroy. I came that they may have life and have it abundantly.

Job 33:28 (HCSB)
He redeemed my soul from going down to the Pit, and I will continue to see the light.

Galatians 4:7 (NLT)
Now you are no longer a slave but God's own child. And since you are his child, God has made you his heir.

325

My child,

Do you believe that you are truly my child? Do you believe that I want the best for your life? Then it's time for you to take off fear of the future and step into your divine destiny. I have not brought you to this place for failure. As I call, will you listen, and respond? Don't jeopardize your journey with me because you fear man. I am with you, move on.

I Love You ~♥~

Ephesians 2:1-6 (MSG)
It wasn't so long ago that you were mired in that old stagnant life of sin. You let the world, which doesn't know the first thing about living, tell you how to live. You filled your lungs with polluted unbelief, and then exhaled disobedience. We all did it, all of us doing what we felt like doing, when we felt like doing it, all of us in the same boat. It's a wonder God didn't lose his temper and do away with the whole lot of us. Instead, immense in mercy and with an incredible love, he embraced us. He took our sin-dead lives and made us alive in Christ. He did all this on his own, with no help from us! Then he picked us up and set us down in highest heaven in company with Jesus, our Messiah.

Romans 8:28 (KJV)
And we know that all things work together for good to them that love God, to them who are the called according to his purpose.

Isaiah 35:4 (AMP)
Say to those with an anxious and panic-stricken heart, "Be strong, fear not! Indeed, your God will come with vengeance [for the ungodly]; The retribution of God will come, But He will save you."

1 Chronicles 28:20 (ESV)
Then David said to Solomon his son, "Be strong and courageous and do it. Do not be afraid and do not be dismayed, for the Lord God, even my God, is with you. He will not leave you or forsake you, until all the work for the service of the house of the Lord is finished.

My child,

Before anyone can love you, they must first love me. True love only comes from me; your Heavenly Father. If you are searching for love in all the wrong places, you will find a counterfeit love. I have the real thing for you and nothing can compare to it. Allow me to love you as you deserve.

I Love You ~♥~

1 John 4:7-8 (AMP)
Beloved, let us [unselfishly] love and seek the best for one another, for love is from God; and everyone who loves [others] is born of God and knows God [through personal experience]. 8 The one who does not love has not become acquainted with God [does not and never did know Him], for God is love. [He is the originator of love, and it is an enduring attribute of His nature.]

1 John 3:1 (HCSB)
Look at how great a love the Father has given us that we should be called God's children. And we are! The reason the world does not know us is that it didn't know Him.

Deuteronomy 7:9-10 (ESV)
Know therefore that the Lord your God is God, the faithful God who keeps covenant and steadfast love with those who love him and keep his commandments, to a thousand generations, 10 and repays to their face those who hate him, by destroying them. He will not be slack with one who hates him. He will repay him to his face.

John 13:34-35 (MSG)
Let me give you a new command: Love one another. In the same way I loved you, you love one another. This is how everyone will recognize that you are my disciples—when they see the love you have for each other.

Colossians 2:6-7 (NLT)
And now, just as you accepted Christ Jesus as your Lord, you must continue to follow him. 7 Let your roots grow down into him, and let your lives be built on him. Then your faith will grow strong in the truth you were taught, and you will overflow with thankfulness.

My child,

When you are ready to let go, I will move you forward. The feeling you have of being stuck is not driven by your circumstances, but how you are allowing them to direct you. Letting go does not say they won, or you did not matter. It is a choice you make and a step you take to move forward. Trust me fully with your next destination. Rise above it all and soar with me.

I Love You ~♥~

Proverbs 4:25-27 (NLT)
Look straight ahead, and fix your eyes on what lies before you. 26 Mark out a straight path for your feet; stay on the safe path. 27 Don't get sidetracked; keep your feet from following evil.

Isaiah 26:3 (AMP)
"You will keep in perfect and constant peace the one whose mind is steadfast [that is, committed and focused on You—in both inclination and character], Because he trusts and takes refuge in You [with hope and confident expectation].

1 Corinthians 13:12 (HCSB)
For now we see indistinctly, as in a mirror, but then face to face. Now I know in part, but then I will know fully, as I am fully known.

Philippians 4:6-7 (MSG)
Don't fret or worry. Instead of worrying, pray. Let petitions and praises shape your worries into prayers, letting God know your concerns. Before you know it, a sense of God's wholeness, everything coming together for good, will come and settle you down. It's wonderful what happens when Christ displaces worry at the center of your life.

Isaiah 40:31 (NASB)
Yet those who wait for the Lord Will gain new strength; They will mount up with wings like eagles, They will run and not get tired, They will walk and not become weary.

My Child,

I Love You

My child,

Stay focused on me. I know your mind is running in so many different directions. If you will settle down and spend time with me, things will get better. When you give me quality time, you will have a quality life. Meditate on my goodness and grace. Spend time in worship and you'll quickly discover worry will leave you. When you truly surrender yourself to me, I will show you the way. Stop looking to things for what you want, and look to me for what you need.

I Love You ~♥~

Psalm 1:1-6 (KJV)
Blessed is the man that walketh not in the counsel of the ungodly, nor standeth in the way of sinners, nor sitteth in the seat of the scornful. 2 But his delight is in the law of the Lord; and in his law doth he meditate day and night. 3 And he shall be like a tree planted by the rivers of water, that bringeth forth his fruit in his season; his leaf also shall not wither; and whatsoever he doeth shall prosper. 4 The ungodly are not so: but are like the chaff which the wind driveth away. 5 Therefore the ungodly shall not stand in the judgment, nor sinners in the congregation of the righteous.   6 For the Lord knoweth the way of the righteous: but the way of the ungodly shall perish.

Colossians 2:6-10 (MSG)
6-7 My counsel for you is simple and straightforward: Just go ahead with what you've been given. You received Christ Jesus, the Master; now live him. You're deeply rooted in him. You're well-constructed upon him. You know your way around the faith. Now do what you've been taught. School's out; quit studying the subject and start living it! And let your living spill over into thanksgiving. 8-10 Watch out for people who try to dazzle you with big words and intellectual double-talk. They want to drag you off into endless arguments that never amount to anything. They spread their ideas through the empty traditions of human beings and the empty superstitions of spirit beings. But that's not the way of Christ. Everything of God gets expressed in him, so you can see and hear him clearly. You don't need a telescope, a microscope, or a horoscope to realize the fullness of Christ, and the emptiness of the universe without him. When you come to him, that fullness comes together for you, too. His power extends over everything.

My child,
When you follow me and walk in my path, even in times of turmoil, you will have peace. This peace does not come from possessions, people, power or positions; it comes directly from me. Abide in my will, and you will find the way, the truth and the life I have prepared for you.

I Love You ~♥~

Psalm 25:10 (MSG)
From now on every road you travel will take you to God. Follow the Covenant signs; Read the charted directions.

Jeremiah 6:16 (ESV)
Thus says the Lord: "Stand by the roads, and look, and ask for the ancient paths, where the good way is; and walk in it, and find rest for your souls. But they said, 'We will not walk in it.'

Psalm 17:6 (HCSB)
I call on You, God, because You will answer me; listen closely to me; hear what I say.

Psalm 25:4 (NASB)
Make me know Your ways, O Lord; Teach me Your paths.

John 8:12 (AMP)
Once more Jesus addressed the crowd. He said, "I am the Light of the world. He who follows Me will not walk in the darkness, but will have the Light of life."

John 14:6 (NLT)
Jesus told him, "I am the way, the truth, and the life. No one can come to the Father except through me."

My child,

The tide is changing and you must flow in my Spirit. Be willing to go where I send you, for I have called you forth. I have Kingdom work for you, and you are the only one that can do what I've called you to do. My favor is upon all who say "yes" to me, and walk in obedience. Your greatest days are ahead of you - walk in victory, my child!

I Love You ~♥~

Ezekiel 36:26-28 (AMP)
Moreover, I will give you a new heart and put a new spirit within you, and I will remove the heart of stone from your flesh and give you a heart of flesh. 27 I will put my Spirit within you and cause you to walk in My statutes, and you will keep My ordinances and do them. 28 You will live in the land that I gave to your fathers; and you will be My people, and I will be your God.

Ephesians 1:4-6 (ESV)
...even as he chose us in him before the foundation of the world, that we should be holy and blameless before him. In love 5 he predestined us for adoption as sons through Jesus Christ, according to the purpose of his will, 6 to the praise of his glorious grace, with which he has blessed us in the Beloved.

Deuteronomy 30:1-6 (NIV)
When all these blessings and curses I have set before you come on you and you take them to heart wherever the LORD your God disperses you among the nations, 2 and when you and your children return to the LORD your God and obey him with all your heart and with all your soul according to everything I command you today, 3 then the LORD your God will restore your fortunes and have compassion on you and gather you again from all the nations where he scattered you. 4 Even if you have been banished to the most distant land under the heavens, from there the LORD your God will gather you and bring you back. 5 He will bring you to the land that belonged to your ancestors, and you will take possession of it. He will make you more prosperous and numerous than your ancestors. 6 The LORD your God will circumcise your hearts and the hearts of your descendants, so that you may love him with all your heart and with all your soul, and live.

My child,
Time and time again I've tried to get your attention and show you my marvelous works. The fear and doubt you are carrying in your heart is blocking your ability to experience the fullness of my presence in your life. You must remove it and make room for me. Fear tells you everything that could go wrong; faith says trust me; everything is right! I Love You ~♥~

Psalm 139:14 (KJV)
I will praise thee; for I am fearfully and wonderfully made: marvellous are thy works; and that my soul knoweth right well.

Psalm 92:5 (AMP)
How great are Your works, O Lord! Your thoughts are very deep [beyond man's understanding].

Psalm 105:1-3 (HCSB)
Give thanks to Yahweh, call on His name; proclaim His deeds among the peoples.2 Sing to Him, sing praise to Him; tell about all His wonderful works! 3 Honor His holy name;let the hearts of those who seek Yahweh rejoice.

John 14:27 (ESV)
Peace I leave with you; my peace I give to you. Not as the world gives do I give to you. Let not your hearts be troubled, neither let them be afraid.

Isaiah 35:3-4 (MSG)
Energize the limp hands, strengthen the rubbery knees. Tell fearful souls, "Courage! Take heart! God is here, right here, on his way to put things right And redress all wrongs. He's on his way! He'll save you!"

Joshua 1:9 (NLT)
This is my command—be strong and courageous! Do not be afraid or discouraged. For the Lord your God is with you wherever you go.

Psalm 56:3 (NIV)
When I am afraid, I put my trust in you.

My child,

Victory belongs to you through me. When you abide in my will and walk in my ways, you will be victorious. Don't measure with worldly standards, it will not add up. My kingdom is beyond this world, and cannot be explained. Trust me, walk it out and watch me work.

I Love You ~♥~

Deuteronomy 20:4 (AMP)
...for the Lord your God is He who goes with you, to fight for you against your enemies, to save you.

Psalm 3:8 (KJV)
Salvation belongeth unto the Lord: thy blessing is upon thy people. Selah.

1 John 5:4 (ESV)
For everyone who has been born of God overcomes the world. And this is the victory that has overcome the world—our faith.

Romans 8:31 (HCSB)
What then are we to say about these things? If God is for us, who is against us?

Proverbs 21:31 (NLT)
The horse is prepared for the day of battle, but the victory belongs to the Lord.

1 Corinthians 15:57 (NIV)
But thanks be to God! He gives us the victory through our Lord Jesus Christ.

My Child,

_____

_____

_____

_____

_____

_____

_____

_____

_____

_____

_____

_____

_____

_____

_____

_____

_____

_____

_____

_____

_____

_____

_____

_____

_____

_____

_____

_____

_____

I Love You

~ ~

IS IT A good IDEA or a job idea?

My child,

Why do you fill your mind with fear? I tell you in my word over and over to fear not! Why are you living in fear? Do you not believe my words? Do you place more confidence in man than me? I am speaking to you now, do not fear! I am in control. Faith builds you up; fear tears you down. Release your fears and replace it with faith.

I Love You ~♥~

Philippians 4:6-7 (NIV)
Do not be anxious about anything, but in every situation, by prayer and petition, with thanksgiving, present your requests to God. 7 And the peace of God, which transcends all understanding, will guard your hearts and your minds in Christ Jesus.

2 Timothy 1:7 (HCSB)
For God has not given us a spirit of fearfulness, but one of power, love, and sound judgment.

Psalm 94:19 (AMP)
When my anxious thoughts multiply within me, Your comforts delight me.

Isaiah 43:1-3 (NLT)
But now, O Jacob, listen to the Lord who created you. O Israel, the one who formed you says, "Do not be afraid, for I have ransomed you. I have called you by name; you are mine. 2 When you go through deep waters, I will be with you. When you go through rivers of difficulty, you will not drown. When you walk through the fire of oppression, you will not be burned up; the flames will not consume you. 3 For I am the Lord, your God, the Holy One of Israel, your Savior. I gave Egypt as a ransom for your freedom; I gave Ethiopia and Seba in your place.

1 Peter 5:6-7 (MSG)
So be content with who you are, and don't put on airs. God's strong hand is on you; he'll promote you at the right time. Live carefree before God; he is most careful with you.

My child,

The steps you are taking will usher in a deeper anointing on your life. Anytime you are moving in my Spirit you will experience my power flowing through you. I will bring great revelation to you and show you things you never thought possible. Stay focused and faithful - just keep moving with me.

I Love You ~♥~

Luke 4:18-19 (ESV)
"The Spirit of the Lord is upon me, because he has anointed me to proclaim good news to the poor. He has sent me to proclaim liberty to the captives and recovering of sight to the blind, to set at liberty those who are oppressed, 19 to proclaim the year of the Lord's favor."

1 John 2:20 (HCSB)
But you have an anointing from the Holy One, and all of you have knowledge.

Acts 10:38 (KJV)
How God anointed Jesus of Nazareth with the Holy Ghost and with power: who went about doing good, and healing all that were oppressed of the devil; for God was with him.

Ephesians 1:15-19 (MSG)
That's why, when I heard of the solid trust you have in the Master Jesus and your outpouring of love to all the followers of Jesus, I couldn't stop thanking God for you—every time I prayed, I'd think of you and give thanks. But I do more than thank. I ask—ask the God of our Master, Jesus Christ, the God of glory—to make you intelligent and discerning in knowing him personally, your eyes focused and clear, so that you can see exactly what it is he is calling you to do, grasp the immensity of this glorious way of life he has for his followers, oh, the utter extravagance of his work in us who trust him—endless energy, boundless strength!

My child,

In my economy, things may not always add up the same. I can make more out of your less. It's not for you to understand. When you place everything - your finances, your family, your faith - your entire life in my hands, you are agreeing to my terms. Trust me and know that I am always working everything for the good. It may not feel good at the time, but the results will always be good.

I Love You ~♥~

John 3:30 (ESV)
He must increase, but I must decrease.

Romans 12:1 (NIV)
Therefore, I urge you, brothers and sisters, in view of God's mercy, to offer your bodies as a living sacrifice, holy and pleasing to God—this is your true and proper worship.

Job 11:13-15 (HCSB)
As for you, if you redirect your heart and lift up your hands to Him in prayer - 14 if there is iniquity in your hand, remove it, and don't allow injustice to dwell in your tents - 15 then you will hold your head high, free from fault. You will be firmly established and unafraid.

Galatians 2:20 (AMP)
I have been crucified with Christ [that is, in Him I have shared His crucifixion]; it is no longer I who live, but Christ lives in me. The life I now live in the body I live by faith [by adhering to, relying on, and completely trusting] in the Son of God, who loved me and gave Himself up for me.

Mark 8:34-37 (MSG)
Calling the crowd to join his disciples, he said, "Anyone who intends to come with me has to let me lead. You're not in the driver's seat; I am. Don't run from suffering; embrace it. Follow me and I'll show you how. Self-help is no help at all. Self-sacrifice is the way, my way, to saving yourself, your true self. What good would it do to get everything you want and lose you, the real you? What could you ever trade your soul for?

My child,

It's time for you to revisit past hurts, and see if you are holding on to unforgiveness. Don't try and justify yourself or make excuses, but truly search your heart. When you choose to hold on to an offense, it blocks my free-flowing forgiveness in your heart. Ask me if there is anything you need to place under the blood of Jesus. Forgiveness sets you free!

I Love You ~♥~

Matthew 18:21-35 (NLT)
Then Peter came to him and asked, "Lord, how often should I forgive someone who sins against me? Seven times?" 22 "No, not seven times," Jesus replied, "but seventy times seven! 23 Therefore, the Kingdom of Heaven can be compared to a king who decided to bring his accounts up to date with servants who had borrowed money from him. 24 In the process, one of his debtors was brought in who owed him millions of dollars. 25 He couldn't pay, so his master ordered that he be sold—along with his wife, his children, and everything he owned—to pay the debt. 26 "But the man fell down before his master and begged him, 'Please, be patient with me, and I will pay it all.' 27 Then his master was filled with pity for him, and he released him and forgave his debt. 28 "But when the man left the king, he went to a fellow servant who owed him a few thousand dollars. He grabbed him by the throat and demanded instant payment. 29 "His fellow servant fell down before him and begged for a little more time. 'Be patient with me, and I will pay it,' he pleaded. 30 But his creditor wouldn't wait. He had the man arrested and put in prison until the debt could be paid in full. 31 "When some of the other servants saw this, they were very upset. They went to the king and told him everything that had happened. 32 Then the king called in the man he had forgiven and said, 'You evil servant! I forgave you that tremendous debt because you pleaded with me. 33 Shouldn't you have mercy on your fellow servant, just as I had mercy on you?' 34 Then the angry king sent the man to prison to be tortured until he had paid his entire debt. 35 "That's what my heavenly Father will do to you if you refuse to forgive your brothers and sisters from your heart."

My child,

When your heart is full of me, there is no room available for the enemy to enter in, and the enemy of your soul will not have access. Today, I am asking you to take a look deep within your heart; see if you have any bitterness, unconfessed sin or strife in your heart. Ask me to remove all the filth from your heart. The devil will not dwell in clean places - he likes darkness and dirt!

I Love You ~♥~

Hebrews 10:22 (AMP)
...let us approach [God] with a true and sincere heart in unqualified assurance of faith, having had our hearts sprinkled clean from an evil conscience and our bodies washed with pure water.

Psalm 97:11 (KJV)
Light is sown for the righteous, and gladness for the upright in heart.

Psalm 24:4 (HCSB)
The one who has clean hands and a pure heart, who has not set his mind on what is false, and who has not sworn deceitfully.

Matthew 5:8 (MSG)
"You're blessed when you get your inside world—your mind and heart—put right. Then you can see God in the outside world.

Isaiah 5:20 (NASB)
Woe to those who call evil good, and good evil; Who substitute darkness for light and light for darkness; Who substitute bitter for sweet and sweet for bitter!

1 John 1:6 (NIV)
If we claim to have fellowship with him and yet walk in the darkness, we lie and do not live out the truth.

Romans 13:12 (NLT)
The night is almost gone; the day of salvation will soon be here. So remove your dark deeds like dirty clothes, and put on the shining armor of right living.

My Child,

I Love You

~~

My child,

Why are you so concerned with what others think of you? Is it not enough for you that I know you by name, that I call you mine and claim you as my child? Many times you are disappointed by people because your expectations are not met by them. Well, stop placing unrealistic expectations on people and look to me. I will never fail to meet what you expect of me.

I Love You ~♥~

1 Thessalonians 2:3-5 (MSG)
God tested us thoroughly to make sure we were qualified to be trusted with this Message. Be assured that when we speak to you we're not after crowd approval—only God approval. Since we've been put through that battery of tests, you're guaranteed that both we and the Message are free of error, mixed motives, or hidden agendas. We never used words to butter you up. No one knows that better than you. And God knows we never used words as a smoke screen to take advantage of you.

Colossians 3:23-24 (AMP)
Whatever you do [whatever your task may be], work from the soul [that is, put in your very best effort], as [something done] for the Lord and not for men, 24 knowing [with all certainty] that it is from the Lord [not from men] that you will receive the inheritance which is your [greatest] reward. It is the Lord Christ whom you [actually] serve.

Matthew 6:1-4 (MSG)
"Be especially careful when you are trying to be good so that you don't make a performance out of it. It might be good theater, but the God who made you won't be applauding. 2-4 "When you do something for someone else, don't call attention to yourself. You've seen them in action, I'm sure—'playactors' I call them— treating prayer meeting and street corner alike as a stage, acting compassionate as long as someone is watching, playing to the crowds. They get applause, true, but that's all they get. When you help someone out, don't think about how it looks. Just do it—quietly and unobtrusively. That is the way your God, who conceived you in love, working behind the scenes, helps you out.

My child,

Many times the thoughts you have are influenced by others. Get alone with me and let my thoughts infiltrate your mind. I want to influence you through my word. When you follow my word, you will not pass misguided judgments on others. You will walk in perfect peace and find unspeakable joy. Tell me, who else can do that for you?

I Love You ~♥~

1 Corinthians 15:33 (AMP)
Do not be deceived: "Bad company corrupts good morals."

Colossians 4:6 (ESV)
Let your speech always be gracious, seasoned with salt, so that you may know how you ought to answer each person.

Acts 24:16 (HCSB)
I always do my best to have a clear conscience toward God and men.

Romans 12:2 (KJV)
And be not conformed to this world: but be ye transformed by the renewing of your mind, that ye may prove what is that good, and acceptable, and perfect, will of God.

1 Peter 1:6-9 (NLT)
So be truly glad There is wonderful joy ahead, even though you must endure many trials for a little while. 7 These trials will show that your faith is genuine. It is being tested as fire tests and purifies gold—though your faith is far more precious than mere gold. So when your faith remains strong through many trials, it will bring you much praise and glory and honor on the day when Jesus Christ is revealed to the whole world. 8 You love him even though you have never seen him. Though you do not see him now, you trust him; and you rejoice with a glorious, inexpressible joy. 9 The reward for trusting him will be the salvation of your souls.

My child,

Grace is the best place for you to abide. When you give grace, you receive grace. When you walk in grace, it allows me to direct your steps. When you speak in grace, I am in control of your words. Living in grace is a beautiful place.

I Love You ~♥~

Ephesians 4:7 (AMP)
Yet grace [God's undeserved favor] was given to each one of us [not indiscriminately, but in different ways] in proportion to the measure of Christ's [rich and abundant] gift.

Ephesians 2:8-9 (ESV)
For by grace you have been saved through faith. And this is not your own doing; it is the gift of God, 9 not a result of works, so that no one may boast.

2 Peter 1:2 (HCSB)
May grace and peace be multiplied to you through the knowledge of God and of Jesus our Lord.

Hebrews 4:16 (KJV)
Let us therefore come boldly unto the throne of grace, that we may obtain mercy, and find grace to help in time of need.

2 Corinthians 8:7 (NASB)
But just as you abound in everything, in faith and utterance and knowledge and in all earnestness and in the [a]love we inspired in you, see that you abound in this gracious work also.

Luke 6:37-38 (MSG)
"Don't pick on people, jump on their failures, criticize their faults—unless, of course, you want the same treatment. Don't condemn those who are down; that hardness can boomerang. Be easy on people; you'll find life a lot easier. Give away your life; you'll find life given back, but not merely given back—given back with bonus and blessing. Giving, not getting, is the way. Generosity begets generosity."

My child,

There are areas of your life that are entangled with worldly snares. If you will invite me into those areas, I will begin to free you from the bondage that entraps you. I came so you could live victoriously through me. You must trust, obey and believe me. You are no longer a slave - you are free!

I Love You ~♥~

Galatians 5:1 (AMP)
It was for this freedom that Christ set us free [completely liberating us]; therefore keep standing firm and do not be subject again to a yoke of slavery [which you once removed].

Romans 8:21 (HCSB)
...that the creation itself will also be set free from the bondage of corruption into the glorious freedom of God's children.

2 Peter 2:20 (KJV)
For if after they have escaped the pollutions of the world through the knowledge of the Lord and Saviour Jesus Christ, they are again entangled therein, and overcome, the latter end is worse with them than the beginning.

Luke 6:46-49 (MSG)
"Why are you so polite with me, always saying 'Yes, sir,' and 'That's right, sir,' but never doing a thing I tell you? These words I speak to you are not mere additions to your life, homeowner improvements to your standard of living. They are foundation words, words to build a life on. 48-49 "If you work the words into your life, you are like a smart carpenter who dug deep and laid the foundation of his house on bedrock. When the river burst its banks and crashed against the house, nothing could shake it; it was built to last. But if you just use my words in Bible studies and don't work them into your life, you are like a dumb carpenter who built a house but skipped the foundation. When the swollen river came crashing in, it collapsed like a house of cards. It was a total loss."

My child,

You have been asking for clarity over your situation. If you will wait on me, I will send the answer. Trust me, don't get in a hurry and try to fix this. Let me have it and take your hands off. When you place it in my hands, then I can help you. Release it to me and I will return your joy!

I Love You ~♥~

1 John 5:14-15 (NLT)
And we are confident that he hears us whenever we ask for anything that pleases him. 15 And since we know he hears us when we make our requests, we also know that he will give us what we ask for.

John 15:5-8 (MSG)
"I am the Vine, you are the branches. When you're joined with me and I with you, the relation intimate and organic, the harvest is sure to be abundant. Separated, you can't produce a thing. Anyone who separates from me is deadwood, gathered up and thrown on the bonfire. But if you make yourselves at home with me and my words are at home in you, you can be sure that whatever you ask will be listened to and acted upon. This is how my Father shows who he is— when you produce grapes, when you mature as my disciples.

Psalm 37:4-5 (NASB)
Delight yourself in the Lord; And He will give you the desires of your heart. 5 Commit your way to the Lord, Trust also in Him, and He will do it.

Micah 7:7 (AMP)
But as for me, I will look expectantly for the Lord and with confidence in Him I will keep watch; I will wait [with confident expectation] for the God of my salvation. My God will hear me.

Philippians 4:6-7 (ESV)
...do not be anxious about anything, but in everything by prayer and supplication with thanksgiving let your requests be made known to God. 7 And the peace of God, which surpasses all understanding, will guard your hearts and your minds in Christ Jesus.

My Child,

_____

_____

_____

_____

_____

_____

_____

_____

_____

_____

_____

_____

_____

_____

_____

_____

_____

_____

_____

_____

_____

_____

_____

I Love You

~ ~

man says

moderation

God says

separation

My child,

Come to me when your heart is heavy and restless. I can make your burdens light and give you rest. Often times your heaviness and restlessness is due to decisions you have made outside of my will. Stop immediately and ask my advice for your life. My way brings peace; the way of man brings pressure. It may even look good, but not be in line with my will for you. Stay close to me and I'll lead you through.

I Love You ~♥~

1 Timothy 6:20-21 (AMP)
O Timothy, guard and keep safe the deposit [of godly truth] entrusted to you, turn away from worldly and godless chatter [with its profane, empty words], and the contradictions of what is falsely called "knowledge"— 21 which some have professed and by doing so have erred (missed the mark) and strayed from the faith.

Isaiah 26:3 (ESV)
You keep him in perfect peace whose mind is stayed on you, because he trusts in you. Grace be with you.

Exodus 33:14 (HCSB)
Then He replied, "My presence will go with you, and I will give you rest."

Jeremiah 6:16 (NLT)
This is what the Lord says: "Stop at the crossroads and look around. Ask for the old, godly way, and walk in it. Travel its path, and you will find rest for your souls. But you reply, 'No, that's not the road we want!'

Matthew 11:28-30 (MSG)
"Are you tired? Worn out? Burned out on religion? Come to me. Get away with me and you'll recover your life. I'll show you how to take a real rest. Walk with me and work with me—watch how I do it. Learn the unforced rhythms of grace. I won't lay anything heavy or ill-fitting on you. Keep company with me and you'll learn to live freely and lightly."

My child,

Your struggles are my struggles. How is that possible? When you are carrying burdens in your heart, they create blockages, and my blessings cannot flow. I'm asking you today to examine your heart. Look and see if you are carrying anything that is hindering you from worshipping me. Ask me to release you from worrying over your struggles, and I will strengthen your faith through worship!

I Love You ~♥~

Psalm 9:9-10 (ESV)
The Lord is a stronghold for the oppressed, a stronghold in times of trouble. 10 And those who know your name put their trust in you, for you, O Lord, have not forsaken those who seek you.

Philippians 4:19 (KJV)
But my God shall supply all your need according to his riches in glory by Christ Jesus.

2 Corinthians 4:7-12 (MSG)
If you only look at us, you might well miss the brightness. We carry this precious Message around in the unadorned clay pots of our ordinary lives. That's to prevent anyone from confusing God's incomparable power with us. As it is, there's not much chance of that. You know for yourselves that we're not much to look at. We've been surrounded and battered by troubles, but we're not demoralized; we're not sure what to do, but we know that God knows what to do; we've been spiritually terrorized, but God hasn't left our side; we've been thrown down, but we haven't broken. What they did to Jesus, they do to us—trial and torture, mockery and murder; what Jesus did among them, he does in us—he lives! Our lives are at constant risk for Jesus' sake, which makes Jesus' life all the more evident in us. While we're going through the worst, you're getting in on the best!

Psalm 55:22 (NASB)
Cast your burden upon the Lord and He will sustain you; He will never allow the righteous to be shaken.

My child,
You have opportunities throughout your day to worship me. I am calling the true worshippers to arise. Darkness lingers all around you, trying to consume you. Your worship will break through the darkness and shine my light. When my light breaks forth, truth will be revealed. Dispel darkness and live in the light!

I Love You ~♥~

Romans 12:1 (AMP)
Therefore I urge you, brothers and sisters, by the mercies of God, to present your bodies [dedicating all of yourselves, set apart] as a living sacrifice, holy and well-pleasing to God, which is your rational (logical, intelligent) act of worship.

John 4:23 (ESV)
But the hour is coming, and is now here, when the true worshipers will worship the Father in spirit and truth, for the Father is seeking such people to worship him.

Luke 12:3 (NLT)
Whatever you have said in the dark will be heard in the light, and what you have whispered behind closed doors will be shouted from the housetops for all to hear!

Acts 26:17-18 (MSG)
"'I'm sending you off to open the eyes of the outsiders so they can see the difference between dark and light, and choose light, see the difference between Satan and God, and choose God. I'm sending you off to present my offer of sins forgiven, and a place in the family, inviting them into the company of those who begin real living by believing in me.

Ephesians 5:11 (HCSB)
Don't participate in the fruitless works of darkness, but instead expose them.

My child,

Today begins a new journey for you. This path has been prepared for a long time. I have wonderful things along this path for you. Enjoy your life and find joy in every day. I promise I place joy around you - you just need to look around and embrace it. I am proud of you.

I Love You ~♥~

1 Peter 1:8-9 (AMP)
Though you have not seen Him, you love Him; and though you do not even see Him now, you believe and trust in Him and you greatly rejoice and delight with inexpressible and glorious joy, 9 receiving as the result [the outcome, the consummation] of your faith, the salvation of your souls.

Isaiah 12:6 (ESV)
Shout, and sing for joy, O inhabitant of Zion, for great in your midst is the Holy One of Israel.

Philemon 7 (HCSB)
For I have great joy and encouragement from your love, because the hearts of the saints have been refreshed through you, brother.

Proverbs 15:23 (KJV)
A man hath joy by the answer of his mouth: and a word spoken in due season, how good is it!

Psalm 30:4-5 (MSG)
All you saints! Sing your hearts out to God! Thank him to his face! He gets angry once in a while, but across a lifetime there is only love. The nights of crying your eyes out give way to days of laughter.

Hebrews 12:2 (NLT)
We do this by keeping our eyes on Jesus, the champion who initiates and perfects our faith. Because of the joy awaiting him, he endured the cross, disregarding its shame. Now he is seated in the place of honor beside God's throne.

My child,

When you see things falling apart, do not worry. I am rearranging things and bringing them into my perfect alignment with my will. From time to time everyone needs a readjustment to set things back into order. When you find yourself feeling pressure or frustration, stop and ask me if you are in alignment with your assignment? Then wait and allow me to work my will through your life. You are not alone - I am by your side!

I Love You ~♥~

1 Thessalonians 5:18 (AMP)
... in every situation [no matter what the circumstances] be thankful and continually give thanks to God; for this is the will of God for you in Christ Jesus.

Jeremiah 29:11-13 (ESV)
For I know the plans I have for you, declares the Lord, plans for welfare and not for evil, to give you a future and a hope. 12 Then you will call upon me and come and pray to me, and I will hear you. 13 You will seek me and find me, when you seek me with all your heart.

Hebrews 13:20-21 (HCSB)
Now may the God of peace, who brought up from the dead our Lord Jesus—the great Shepherd of the sheep—with the blood of the everlasting covenant, 21 equip you with all that is good to do His will, working in us what is pleasing in His sight, through Jesus Christ. Glory belongs to Him forever and ever. Amen.

Ephesians 5:15-20 (NLT)
So be careful how you live. Don't live like fools, but like those who are wise. Make the most of every opportunity in these evil days. Don't act thoughtlessly, but understand what the Lord wants you to do. Don't be drunk with wine, because that will ruin your life. Instead, be filled with the Holy Spirit, singing psalms and hymns and spiritual songs among yourselves, and making music to the Lord in your hearts. And give thanks for everything to God the Father in the name of our Lord Jesus Christ.

My Child,

I Love You

Growing Gains bring growing Gains

My child,

When you submit everything to me, your labor is not in vain. It's only when you're pursuing works of the flesh that you feel disappointed and empty. Stop being self- seeking and seek me. I know your circumstances - I am working through them to show you the true way to live. It's not about your position, power or plans. It's about you seeking and submitting to me. I am everything you need!

I Love You ~♥~

Hebrews 13:20-21 (AMP)
Now may the God of peace [the source of serenity and spiritual well-being] who brought up from the dead our Lord Jesus, the great Shepherd of the sheep, through the blood that sealed and ratified the eternal covenant, 21 equip you with every good thing to carry out His will and strengthen you [making you complete and perfect as you ought to be], accomplishing in us that which is pleasing in His sight, through Jesus Christ, to whom be the glory forever and ever. Amen.

Psalm 143:7-10 (MSG)
Hurry with your answer, God! I'm nearly at the end of my rope. Don't turn away; don't ignore me! That would be certain death. If you wake me each morning with the sound of your loving voice, I'll go to sleep each night trusting in you. Point out the road I must travel; I'm all ears, all eyes before you.Save me from my enemies, God— you're my only hope! Teach me how to live to please you, because you're my God. Lead me by your blessed Spirit into cleared and level pastureland.

John 5:30 (KJV)
I can of mine own self do nothing: as I hear, I judge: and my judgment is just; because I seek not mine own will, but the will of the Father which hath sent me.

Ephesians 6:6--8 (ESV)
...not by the way of eye-service, as people-pleasers, but as bondservants of Christ, doing the will of God from the heart, 7 rendering service with a good will as to the Lord and not to man, 8 knowing that whatever good anyone does, this he will receive back from the Lord, whether he is a bondservant or is free.

My child,
Why are you arguing over my boundaries? If you love me - keep my commandments. Your obedience to me is more important than you being right in man's eyes. Your love for me must be stronger than hatred toward them. I will ask this question to you...do you love me more? If yes, then lay down your rights and let me repair what's wrong. Letting go says you want me more!

I Love You ~♥~

Jeremiah 5:22 (NLT)
Have you no respect for me? Why don't you tremble in my presence? I, the Lord, define the ocean's sandy shoreline as an everlasting boundary that the waters cannot cross. The waves may toss and roar, but they can never pass the boundaries I set.

Psalm 16:6 (AMP)
The [boundary] lines [of the land] have fallen for me in pleasant places; Indeed, my heritage is beautiful to me.

1 John 5:2-4 (ESV)
By this we know that we love the children of God, when we love God and obey his commandments. 3 For this is the love of God, that we keep his commandments. And his commandments are not burdensome. 4 For everyone who has been born of God overcomes the world. And this is the victory that has overcome the world—our faith.

Deuteronomy 6:5 (MSG)
Love God, your God, with your whole heart: love him with all that's in you, love him with all you've got!

1 John 2:15-17 (NASB)
Do not love the world nor the things in the world. If anyone loves the world, the love of the Father is not in him. 16 For all that is in the world, the lust of the flesh and the lust of the eyes and the boastful pride of life, is not from the Father, but is from the world. 17 The world is passing away, and also its lusts; but the one who does the will of God lives forever.

My child,

It is time for you to embrace who I've called you to be in my Kingdom. When you acknowledge your true identity in me, it's no longer about you. I have placed within you gifts for the advancement of my Kingdom work. Seek my face and find your place to pour my love out on others. As you pour, you will be filled!

I Love You ~♥~

John1:12 (AMP)
But to as many as did receive and welcome Him, He gave the right [the authority, the privilege] to become children of God, that is, to those who believe in (adhere to, trust in, and rely on) His name—

Romans 15:7 (ESV)
Therefore welcome one another as Christ has welcomed you, for the glory of God.

1 Peter 2:9-10 (MSG)
But you are the ones chosen by God, chosen for the high calling of priestly work, chosen to be a holy people, God's instruments to do his work and speak out for him, to tell others of the night-and-day difference he made for you—from nothing to something, from rejected to accepted.

1 Peter 4:10 (NASB)
As each one has received a special gift, employ it in serving one another as good stewards of the manifold grace of God.

Luke 6:38 (NKJV)
"Give, and it will be given to you: good measure, pressed down, shaken together, and running over will be put into your bosom. For with the same measure that you use, it will be measured back to you."

John 12:26 (NLT)
Anyone who wants to serve me must follow me, because my servants must be where I am. And the Father will honor anyone who serves me.

My child,

Do not allow circumstances to take your peace from you. When you find yourself facing difficulties, don't despair, look to me to show you greater opportunities in the Spirit. I am calling you to live by my Spirit, not your flesh. When you abide, you will not strive. Live for me in all that you do and follow through the Holy Spirit.

I Love You ~♥~

Romans 5:3-5 (AMP)
And not only this, but [with joy] let us exult in our sufferings and rejoice in our hardships, knowing that hardship (distress, pressure, trouble) produces patient endurance; 4 and endurance, proven character (spiritual maturity); and proven character, hope and confident assurance [of eternal salvation]. 5 Such hope [in God's promises] never disappoints us, because God's love has been abundantly poured out within our hearts through the Holy Spirit who was given to us.

Philippians 4:19 (ESV)
And my God will supply every need of yours according to his riches in glory in Christ Jesus.

Galatians 5:16-17 (NLT)
So I say, let the Holy Spirit guide your lives. Then you won't be doing what your sinful nature craves. 17 The sinful nature wants to do evil, which is just the opposite of what the Spirit wants. And the Spirit gives us desires that are the opposite of what the sinful nature desires. These two forces are constantly fighting each other, so you are not free to carry out your good intentions.

1 John 2:4-6 (MSG)
If someone claims, "I know him well!" but doesn't keep his commandments, he's obviously a liar. His life doesn't match his words. But the one who keeps God's word is the person in whom we see God's mature love. This is the only way to be sure we're in God. Anyone who claims to be intimate with God ought to live the same kind of life Jesus lived.

My child,

If you will fully surrender your schedule to me, I will help manage your time. I have called you to peace not pressure. Take a step back and examine your schedule; then make adjustments. You must be intentional to spend time with me or the enemy will steal it from me. I enjoy having your undivided attention. When you include me in your day; I will lead the way!

I Love You ~♥~

Psalm 31:15 (AMP)
My times are in Your hands; Rescue me from the hand of my enemies and from those who pursue and persecute me.

Psalm 90:12 (ESV)
So teach us to number our days that we may get a heart of wisdom.

James 4:13-15 (HCSB)
Come now, you who say, "Today or tomorrow we will travel to such and such a city and spend a year there and do business and make a profit." 14 You don't even know what tomorrow will bring—what your life will be! For you are like smoke that appears for a little while, then vanishes. 15 Instead, you should say, "If the Lord wills, we will live and do this or that."

Ephesians 5:11-16 (MSG)
Don't waste your time on useless work, mere busywork, the barren pursuits of darkness. Expose these things for the sham they are. It's a scandal when people waste their lives on things they must do in the darkness where no one will see. Rip the cover off those frauds and see how attractive they look in the light of Christ.
Wake up from your sleep, Climb out of your coffins; Christ will show you the light! So watch your step. Use your head. Make the most of every chance you get. These are desperate times!

Proverbs 16:3 (NLT)
Commit your actions to the Lord, and your plans will succeed.

My Child,

_____

_____

_____

_____

_____

_____

_____

_____

_____

_____

_____

_____

_____

_____

_____

_____

_____

_____

_____

_____

_____

_____

_____

_____

_____

_____

_____

I Love You

~ ~

God can
Reverse
the
Curse

My child,

Run to me and you will find refuge. The enemy is all around you, but fear not, you shall not be shaken or moved. Stand firm and do not waver from my divine destiny for your life. Each of you must quiet other voices to hear me. I will never lie to you or lead you astray. Stay in my will and walk in my ways.

I Love You ~♥~

Psalm 46:10 (ESV)
Be still, and know that I am God. I will be exalted among the nations, I will be exalted in the earth.

Psalm 91:2 (AMP)
I will say of the Lord, "He is my refuge and my fortress, My God, in whom I trust [with great confidence, and on whom I rely]!"

Proverbs 14:26 (HCSB)
In the fear of the Lord one has strong confidence and his children have a refuge.

Exodus 18:23 (NASB)
If you do this thing and God so commands you, then you will be able to endure, and all these people also will go to their place in peace."

Colossians 1:23 (NLT)
But you must continue to believe this truth and stand firmly in it. Don't drift away from the assurance you received when you heard the Good News. The Good News has been preached all over the world, and I, Paul, have been appointed as God's servant to proclaim it.

My child,

I want you to know that I am proud of you. These past weeks I have watched you walk through some very difficult circumstances. You not only followed me, but you exercised your faith, and believed that I was in control. This is not always easy, and I am blessed by your faith in me. As you journey through this life, you will have even more opportunities to hold fast to faith. If you will trust me with all that you have, I will bless you with all that you need. Your faith in me releases my favor in your life.

I Love You ~♥~

Hebrews 10:22-25 (MSG)
So let's do it—full of belief, confident that we're presentable inside and out. Let's keep a firm grip on the promises that keep us going. He always keeps his word. Let's see how inventive we can be in encouraging love and helping out, not avoiding worshiping together as some do but spurring each other on, especially as we see the big Day approaching.

1 Peter 5:9 (NLT)
Stand firm against him, and be strong in your faith. Remember that your family of believers all over the world is going through the same kind of suffering you are.

Ephesians 3:16-19 (AMP)
May He grant you out of the riches of His glory, to be strengthened and spiritually energized with power through His Spirit in your inner self, [indwelling your innermost being and personality], 17 so that Christ may dwell in your hearts through your faith. And may you, having been [deeply] rooted and [securely] grounded in love, 18 be fully capable of comprehending with all the saints (God's people) the width and length and height and depth of His love [fully experiencing that amazing, endless love]; 19 and [that you may come] to know [practically, through personal experience] the love of Christ which far surpasses [mere] knowledge [without experience], that you may be filled up [throughout your being] to all the fullness of God [so that you may have the richest experience of God's presence in your lives, completely filled and flooded with God Himself].

My child,

To walk in victory you must place me first in every area of your life. You must invite me to go before you. In times of turmoil, confusion and stress, check yourself and see if you are getting ahead of me. My methods are different than the world's; oftentimes they will not appear correct in the natural. I am working in the supernatural. Open your supernatural eyes and you will see what I am preparing ahead of you.

I Love You ~♥~

Matthew 6:31-33 (AMP)
Therefore do not worry or be anxious (perpetually uneasy, distracted), saying, 'What are we going to eat?' or 'What are we going to drink?' or 'What are we going to wear?' 32 For the [pagan] Gentiles eagerly seek all these things; [but do not worry,] for your heavenly Father knows that you need them. 33 But first and most importantly seek (aim at, strive after) His kingdom and His righteousness [His way of doing and being right—the attitude and character of God], and all these things will be given to you also.

Proverbs 16:3 (ESV)
Commit your work to the Lord, and your plans will be established.

Philippians 4:13 (HCSB)
I am able to do all things through Him who strengthens me.

Matthew 22:37 (KJV)
Jesus said unto him, Thou shalt love the Lord thy God with all thy heart, and with all thy soul, and with all thy mind.

2 Timothy 3:14-17 (MSG)
But don't let it faze you. Stick with what you learned and believed, sure of the integrity of your teachers—why, you took in the sacred Scriptures with your mother's milk! There's nothing like the written Word of God for showing you the way to salvation through faith in Christ Jesus. Every part of Scripture is God-breathed and useful one way or another—showing us truth, exposing our rebellion, correcting our mistakes, training us to live God's way. Through the Word we are put together and shaped up for the tasks God has for us.

My child,

I am near you. You are not alone without hope. If you will cling to me through your pain, I will comfort you. If through uncertain times you will trust me, I will show you the way. In times of sorrow if you will find hope to hang on, I will strengthen you as you carry on. When you partner with me, you can know I am working everything for your good.

I Love You ~♥~

Psalm 25:16 (AMP)
Turn to me [Lord] and be gracious to me, For I am alone and afflicted.

Deuteronomy 31:8 (ESV)
It is the Lord who goes before you. He will be with you; he will not leave you or forsake you. Do not fear or be dismayed."

2 Corinthians 1:5-6 (HCSB)
For as the sufferings of Christ overflow to us, so through Christ our comfort also overflows. 6 If we are afflicted, it is for your comfort and salvation. If we are comforted, it is for your comfort, which is experienced in your endurance of the same sufferings that we suffer.

1 Peter 5:8-11 (MSG)
Keep a cool head. Stay alert. The Devil is poised to pounce, and would like nothing better than to catch you napping. Keep your guard up. You're not the only ones plunged into these hard times. It's the same with Christians all over the world. So keep a firm grip on the faith. The suffering won't last forever. It won't be long before this generous God who has great plans for us in Christ—eternal and glorious plans they are!—will have you put together and on your feet for good. He gets the last word; yes, he does.

Psalm 30:5 (NKJV)
For His anger is but for a moment, His favor is for life; Weeping may endure for a night, But joy comes in the morning.

Psalm 30:11-12 (NLT)
You have turned my mourning into joyful dancing. You have taken away my clothes of mourning and clothed me with joy, 12 that I might sing praises to you and not be silent. O Lord my God, I will give you thanks forever!

My *child,*
I want you to abide in unity. Look for ways to bring harmony to the body of believers. The enemy works to bring division. You must recognize what he is trying to do, and resist his whispers in the night. When the body is united, it is stronger and can stand together to fight against the real enemy. Allow me to put unity in your community.

I Love You ~♥~

Psalm 133:1 (NASB)
Behold, how good and how pleasant it is For brothers to dwell together in unity!

Romans 12:4-6 (MSG)
In this way we are like the various parts of a human body. Each part gets its meaning from the body as a whole, not the other way around. The body we're talking about is Christ's body of chosen people. Each of us finds our meaning and function as a part of his body. But as a chopped-off finger or cut-off toe we wouldn't amount to much, would we? So since we find ourselves fashioned into all these excellently formed and marvelously functioning parts in Christ's body, let's just go ahead and be what we were made to be, without enviously or pridefully comparing ourselves with each other, or trying to be something we aren't.

Ephesians 2:22 (AMP)
In Him [and in fellowship with one another] you also are being built together into a dwelling place of God in the Spirit.

Acts 4:32 (NIV)
All the believers were one in heart and mind. No one claimed that any of their possessions was their own, but they shared everything they had.

Romans 12:16 (NLT)
Live in harmony with each other. Don't be too proud to enjoy the company of ordinary people. And don't think you know it all!

My Child,

I Love You

~~

Author's Biography

Staci Pealock has a call on her life to share and show the love of the Lord to everyone that comes into her life. For many years she felt discarded and unlovable, but through gaining victory over many hurts, heartaches and habits, she now is experiencing life full of joy as an overcomer. She believes that we all have a God- given calling and purpose that is individual and unique, and those who God calls He equips! Staci has published two books, Back Porch Blessings in 2010, and in April of 2012, a children's book Where I Belong. Staci is known for her quick wit and her "Staci-isms", one of them being: "God is LARGE and in CHARGE!" Staci is a licensed minister and the founder and Director of LAMBS ministry located in Turnerville, Georgia. This is a gathering place for women from all different walks of life to come and get "Spiritually Fit!" Staci and her husband, Todd of 31 years, reside in the mountains of Northeast Georgia. They have two grown children Ansley (husband Jared) and Andrew (wife Mikaela) who make her heart beat a little faster.